Focus,

Not Fear

Focus, *Not Fear*

Ali Brown, M.Ed., CPDT

Tanacacia Press

Published by Tanacacia Press
6127 PA Route 873
Slatington, PA 18080
www.greatcompanions.info

For general information on Tanacacia Press, Great Companions, and Ali Brown, please call 610-737-1550, email tanacacia@aol.com or write to the above address.

ISBN 13: 978-0-9766414-1-4

Cover concept: Ali Brown
Cover design: Pete Smoyer, e-Production
Illustrations and photography: Pete Smoyer
Most photographs and biographies in the "Cast of Characters" chapter of the book were provided by the dogs' owners.
Manufactured in the United States of America

Dedication

This book is dedicated to the memory of my dad, Dr. S.L. Brown, who taught me the meaning of a good work ethic; and to the memory of Montana, who taught me that dogs are cool.

Both were lost recently, are missed greatly, and will never be forgotten.

Contents

Above: The barn, parking area, and pond just before sunset. This is where classes take place, both inside and outside. Below: Pow-wow. The group discusses and plans the evening's events.

For Starters

When I wrote, *Scaredy Dog! Understanding and Rehabilitating Your Reactive Dog*, I knew I was outlining helpful and important information for my new students with fearful and reactive dogs. I had hoped it would also be helpful to others in the dog training community and beyond, but its reception worldwide surprised me. Somehow, I had imagined that the crowded and busy world of the northeastern United States had created a unique set of behavior problems in our dogs that dogs in other parts of the world didn't experience. Boy was I wrong! Canine reactivity is, unfortunately, ubiquitous. From New York to San Diego, from London to Johannesburg, there are dogs for whom life is scary and threatening. These dogs needed help, and I'm glad that I have been able to chip in by providing support and recommendations for their owners.

Since writing that book, many other trainers have also started their own classes for reactive dogs. Some call it "rowdy rovers"; others call it "growl class." Whatever they call it, more and more trainers are using positive reinforcement and careful management techniques to help dogs and their people to be more able to work together as a team, lower stress levels, and learn new skills that enable them to deal with reactive triggers in the dogs' lives. Whereas using **positive punishment** and **flooding** were once the norm, these new, more positive techniques are taking their place. Quite a few colleagues of mine have also offered books on similar topics, thereby adding to the wealth of knowledge that we have as a group. This is wonderful news! Our dogs are finally getting the help they need!

Soon after *Scaredy Dog!* was published, I took to the road, offering seminars for trainers and pet owners on the topic of reactivity. I found so many trainers who wanted desperately to help their students but didn't have a framework in which to work. They understood the concepts of **positive reinforcement** and **negative punishment**, but didn't know how to start effectively using them within a class structure. So I would spend as much time as I could, before or after the seminar, and sometimes the next day, and almost always online with them after I went home, giving suggestions and mentoring them so that they could help their students. I love this part of my work as a trainer; it's really very fulfilling to be able to share knowledge with others in my field. But I realize that this information, too, should be put on paper so that everyone can read it, learn it, and understand it so that they may use it and build on it. After all, there are many areas of the country, and I'm sure in the world, where a positive trainer is not within driving distance.

The following pages are my offering to owners who have started to work with their reactive dog or trainers who want to help those with a reactive dog. This book should not be the sole introduction to reactivity, but should follow an introductory book such as *Scaredy Dog!* Training is not the sort of thing that can utilize a cookie-cutter program. There are hundreds of nuances in each individual case, but I have put on paper the best that I have to offer folks who want the best for their reactive dogs.

He's a Great Dog...
Most of the Time

This is what I usually hear on the phone or read in an email from a prospective student. A distraught and desperate person contacts me, sometimes clearly frustrated that they got stuck with a dog with irritating problems, but more often wanting suggestions, input, and help with the dog they love so much. More often than not, I'll hear that phrase or one like it: "He's such a good dog. We love him to pieces. He's great most of the time, but once in a while he goes after someone, or when he sees another dog on a walk, he lunges and barks." The more I speak with the person, the more evidence I get...the walk in the park, the package delivery person, the neighbor's kid coming onto the driveway, the brother-in-law coming into the house wearing a hooded sweatshirt. "Oh yeah, and he barks like crazy when he's in the car and someone walks by while we're at a traffic light. Oh, and one more thing...he goes after trucks. And bikes. Actually, anything with wheels." Sigh.

If you're reading this book, chances are that you're familiar with the term **reactivity**. Just in case you're not, let's define it. Reactivity is sort of a nebulous term, and different trainers have different definitions. For the most part, however, reactivity is offensive-defensive behavior which is based in anxiety and/or fear. The dog shows reactions to stimuli which are greater than we would think necessary -- yes, this is a very subjective measure. The behavior often looks like aggression; that is to say, he barks, lunges, growls, pulls toward the stimulus if on leash. Most of the time, however, given the opportunity to actually get to the stimulus, the dog will retreat or will not know what to do.

Let me give you an example. One night in reactive class, I had my dog, Acacia, with me and was getting her out of the car. Linda had gotten Bailey out of the car (these are all characters you'll get to know soon) and was coming around the corner of the building. Bailey saw Acacia and immediately began to growl and lunge, when suddenly the leash broke! It snapped in two!!!

Bailey ran full steam ahead, directly toward Acacia, as I was blocking for her. When Bailey got to her, he did about four seconds' worth of loud grumbling and hopping around her, as if he was going to jump on her. By then, Linda had caught up to him and taken him by the collar, while I put Acacia back in the car (with a million treats). Afterward we talked at length about it. It was really clear to me that Bailey had no idea what to do…it was all bluff. Bailey's behavior is very typical for a reactive dog. His motto is, "Put on a big front to make the scary thing go away."

The intent of a reactive dog is not to harm others, but to protect himself. A reactive dog acts out of self-preservation, but a dog who has been reactive for a long time is more likely to actually become aggressive than one who is just beginning to become reactive. This may be because the offensive stances that the dog has taken have worked, so he has begun to believe in himself. There's lots of discussion among trainers as to whether a dog is reactive or aggressive, and I think the reason for this is that it is a continuum. This is also why the term **reactivity** is nebulous. Some trainers will consider reactive dogs to be aggressive and will not take on the case. Others will put a reactive dog in a class for aggressive dogs. Regardless of the level of intensity of reactivity, the treatment should be the same.

Simply put, a reactive dog needs to learn that he's not out there on his own. He needs to learn that all good things come from his person, that his person has access to all of the things that he considers valuable, that he and his person together make a great team, and that when in doubt, he should TRUST his person, check in with his person and let his person make all of the important decisions for him. He also needs to learn that being with his person outside on a leash is a privilege, and that if he doesn't pay attention or check in, or if he barks, the privilege goes away. It takes time and practice for creatures on both ends of the leash to learn this new set of rules, and it's easy to make lots of mistakes, but the payoffs are wonderful.

If there is one basic tenet that I wish to make painfully clear to the novice reactive dog owner, it is this: *your dog is reactive 24/7*. There is no downtime for reactivity. You may think that your dog is fine at home when there's nobody else around and that he only has a hard time when he sees another dog while on the leash, but this is not true. To your dog, it's a full time issue. Physiologically, your dog is reactive. It's a systemic problem. Consider it an illness if you need that concept to help you understand it. The body of a reactive dog exists in a state of chronic stress. This stress may have been caused by poor nutrition, poor socialization, lack of exercise, a single traumatic event or series of traumatic events, poor genetics, illness, or a combination of these. There is little reason to feel guilty about the causes, since this does no good but only harm. The important concept here to understand is that you have a dog with a stress issue, and you need to take certain steps to ensure that his stress level is, at all times, as low as possible. ***This means that his behavior and environment needs to be closely monitored and managed in the home, in the car, on walks, at the vet, with visitors, etc. There are no exceptions to this rule!*** Students who begin to make exceptions, or those who make excuses, inevitably experience a lack of progress or a certain loss of progress gained. You can bet that this is quite frustrating for me!

I'd like to give you a simple example of this loss of management, one of which I have been guilty in my early days of working with my own reactive dog, Acacia. A student will come into class and work her dog for a few minutes and be very happy with the dog's focus on her. When she is finished and ready to take the dog back to the car, she stops to ask a question, leaving her attention from her dog. The dog, meanwhile, senses that his person is no longer paying attention to him, and perceives himself as being on his own and needing to make his own decisions. Because of this (or simply because he has nothing else to do), he starts to react to the stimuli in his environment – the very stimuli on which the person had been working him! So the person just took one step forward and two steps back. Frustrating, no?

The obvious solution to this, of course, is to put the dog away in his car or crate first and then come back and ask questions. Your primary directive is to take care of your dog first and foremost, ANY time you and your dog are together on a leash or in an environment where he might be reactive. Your attention MUST to be toward the dog in these situations, over and above anything else which might be going on, even if it means that you can't stop to talk to someone. If you can't focus on your dog, your dog has no reason to focus on you. If your attention must go elsewhere, manage your dog by putting him in an environment in which he is safe, whether that be a car, crate, behind a baby gate or fence, etc. Having said this, let's turn our attention to the specifics of the physical environment.

In the Physical Realm

It seems to me that the most difficult aspect to working a reactive dog or running a class for reactive dogs is where to start. As a trainer, the process begins for me when I get that email or phone call. First, I must decide whether the dog is reactive or aggressive. I personally will work with a dog-aggressive dog but not a person-aggressive dog. My experience is that dog-aggressive dogs have a lower success rate in retraining than reactive dogs because they are more likely to do damage which results in their relinquishment or euthanasia. I do not like to work with person-aggressive dogs because I feel that there are other professionals, namely veterinary behaviorists, who are better prepared to take on such cases.

Once I've decided whether I'll work with a dog, we start with three private lessons. During these lessons, I do a detailed evaluation, discuss exercise, nutrition, management, vaccination, and other holistic topics, and begin to follow the protocols in the *Scaredy Dog!* book. The dog's progress at the third lesson determines the next step for the dog. Sometimes more lessons are on order, sometimes the person decides to go it alone, and sometimes the person wants to begin the reactive class. If this is the case, that person comes to observe a reactive dog class without his dog. At that time, the classmates give a brief explanation of their dogs' issues, and the visiting student acts as **live bait**.

"Oh my God!" you say. "What can she mean by this??" It's a little bit of sick humor thrown into the classes to help us stay sane. All that is meant by this is that people who are not regular visitors to the class are often viewed suspiciously by the dogs who are in the class, so the stimulus level afforded by the visitor is often much higher than the stimulus level of a regularly-attending student. The visitor usually does nothing other than watch and soak in the information, but occasionally, he will be asked to toss a treat to a dog or stand or sit in a particular location (usually far away from the dog being worked).

As you are about to learn, the setup for these classes is unusual, and a person needs to witness it firsthand before coming to the class with his dog.

There are few requirements for selecting an appropriate space in which to run a reactive dog class, but the ones I'm about to list are of extreme importance:

1. *A large space*! Dogs who react to things in their environment will react more intensely if the stimulus is in close proximity to him than if it is farther away. I have run classes in a multitude of locations, including a training studio on the second floor of a mall, the parking lot of that same mall, the parking lot of a middle school (off hours, of course), the parking lot of a swimming club, the parking lot of a little-used park, a child day care (off hours), the front of my house in a neighborhood, and now, my 6.5 acre property. Some of these places were really pretty awful! We have had to contend with trains, planes, helicopters, lightening (which ends class immediately), lack of heat, feral cats, small rooms, unexpected canine visitors, drag racing cars, the sounds of pneumatic drills, lost people coming to ask for directions…you name it! But the most difficult situation is to have a dog in an area which is so tight that he feels trapped and ask him to pay attention to you. While most of the time I disagree with the American adage, "bigger is better," in this case, I agree!

2. *Ample parking for cars*. The way I run my classes is peculiar because the dogs stay in their cars for most of the class. They are kept in their cars because we want the dogs to calmly remain in their familiar environment, away from distracting stimuli. This allows the dogs to have some good "down-time" in between their sessions. Down-time helps them to relax, to reduce their stress levels, and to mentally process what they just learned. The best case scenario involves a dog who is crated in his car. The car is parked away from other cars and not in a place where the dog can hear or see the stimuli which set him off. If proximity is an issue (which it almost always is), the dog can be crated and the crate covered in such a way that the dog can't see out the windows and bark at the other dogs or people. If the dog is not crated in the car, then the car must be covered with blankets, towels, sheets, sun visors, or some other material which blocks the vision of the dog. We will discuss this in more detail later.

3. *Minimum of distractions*. We want to provide our own distractions, with control, to our dogs. We would rather not have other distractions present themselves! Of course, this can be difficult to do. We want to control just about every variable for a newer student; as the person and dog team become more comfortable and more able to handle distractions, unexpected distractions can become a welcome surprise because the person needs to be able to handle almost any situation thrown at her. But the more we are able to control what stimuli will be present, the more successful we will be with our dogs.

4. *Barriers, natural and otherwise*. When we work inside, we have doors, corners, walls, and visual barriers (PVC frames with plastic shower curtains hanging from them) which we use to control the appearance and disappearance of both the dogs and the distractions/stimuli. When we are outside, it's nice to have trees, hills, doors, corners, cars, and other solid objects from which things can appear unexpectedly. One of the most difficult situations for any dog or person is the sudden appearance of a person, object or sound. By giving the person and dog team the opportunity to practice what to do in such a case, we are enabling them to be more successful in real life.

5. *A variety of people, dogs, and distractions at our disposal*. Dogs don't generalize well. For this reason, it's best to have both men and women, large and small dogs, dark and light colored dogs, males and females, young and older dogs.

6. *A small class*. The fewer the number of dogs in the class, the more attention can be paid to each dog, and the less likely the dog will become overwhelmed by smells and dogs barking, etc. I like to keep my classes to five dogs; each class runs approximately two hours.

The location of the classes outlined in this book all took place at the Great Companions property. It is a 6.5 acre property with a one acre pond, a two-story 50' x 50' bank barn, a stone farmhouse, a wire mesh-lined split rail fence connecting the two buildings, and open field with a few scattered trees on the remainder of the property. Below is a diagram of the property itself.

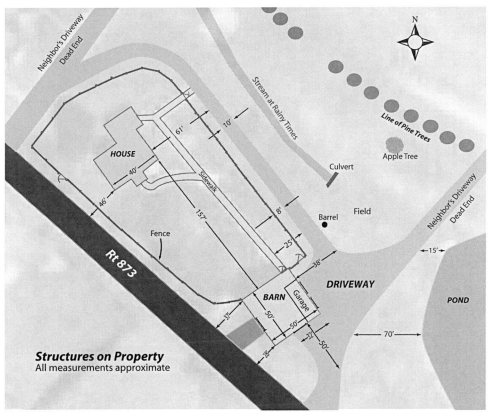

Property Layout. The reactive dog class takes place mostly in the driveway area near the barn's garage. There are two bright sodium vapor lights that keep that area well lit.

As we begin to read about individual classes, this diagram will appear again, with indications of important physical features or movement of dogs and people, so you can see the direction and distance of the activity.

Below is a diagram of the interior portion of the training barn, which we use mostly in very cold or inclement weather.

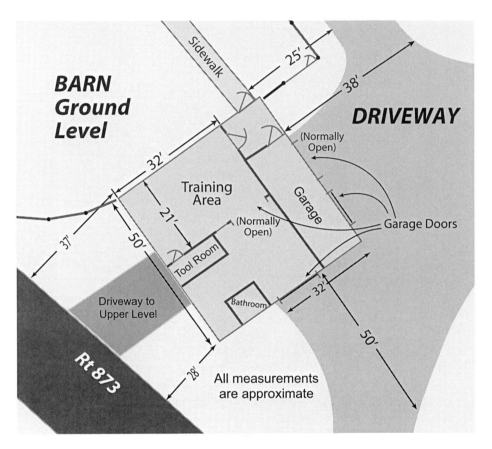

This diagram will also reappear to illustrate positions and movements of people and dogs in certain classes. The Training Area was expanded midway through writing this book.

The Wheel "House"

We use our cars extensively in these reactive classes. They serve as moving homes for our dogs. They provide shelter from cold wind, sun, rain and snow. They prevent our dogs from getting to things to which they react. They allow us to put our dogs away when they are finished working, if they have reacted, or if they are not paying attention to us. The dogs know the car as a familiar place with familiar smells, and should perceive the car as a great place to be. It also allows us to manage our dogs as far away as possible from other dogs in the class, which is something that's usually very difficult to do in a class setting. In a case where an inside space is tremendous, dogs may be maintained in crates, but they must be far enough away that they will not react to each other. When using a crate, the ability to pick up scent may be greater than it would be in a car; this may necessitate an even farther critical distance.

The best setup for the owner of a reactive dog is to have the dog crated in the car. The crate provides safety while driving, and when the car is stationary, the crate can be covered so that the dog can't look out and find things at which to bark. The cover should take the climate into consideration: lightweight but dark colored material in warmer weather, and heavier, dark colored material in colder weather. For warm, sunny days, an aluminum mesh solar blanket can be very helpful.

Problems arise with the use of crates in the car. Too often, I am faced with an owner of a compact car and a full size dog. Crating is not an option, because there simply isn't space for a crate. In these cases, the entire car can be covered on the outside with a sheet, blanket, or some towels. This becomes something of an art, because there is a trade-off between ventilation and providing visual blockage. The covering material can blow off the car, and we often use large magnets on the outside of the car to prevent this from happening. Sometimes, the dog is bored or upset, and pulls the covering inside the car and may chew it. This is a source of real aggravation for the owner, who is simply trying to manage the dog. In these cases, using a harness seatbelt on the dog can help to diminish his ability to move around. We always park our cars so that we can make the most of the natural barriers (and shade) available to us. If I can park my car backed against a wall, I will only need to cover three windows. If I can park tight in the corner of a wall, I will only need to cover two windows.

The most aggravating situation I have to handle with these classes is the

Patti and Tara setting up their car with blankets.

student who will not crate the dog in the car. It's not a matter of inability for these students, it's a matter of inconvenience. The dog is crateable and there is sufficient space in the vehicle, but the student does not wish to buy a crate or spend the money. This is always a shame because the lack of proper management of the dog hampers the dog's success. The dog often finds ways to push the coverings aside, sticks his head out the window (we use the windows as much as we can for ventilation), and finds things to bark at. The dog seems to feel that he has the opportunity to elicit attention by barking, which arouses him and creates a poor reaction from other dogs in the class. Sometimes, this gets all the dogs going, and the productivity of the entire class is lost. This could all be avoided by crating!

Not all dogs are crateable, and not all dogs love their cars. In the former case, it's usually a dog with some level of **separation anxiety**. In the latter case, generalized anxiety is the ruling factor. In both cases, lots of pre-training needs to take place before the dog can join the class and benefit from it. If the dog is panicking while in the car, no learning can take place when he's out of the car working. A discussion of separation anxiety is not within the realm of this book, but there are great resources to help (see the "Resources and Reading" section). If the dog is anxious about the car, you can do some training in the car during the week. Go into the car with the dog and do some **stuff-a-dog**, **targeting**, and other tricks. Feed your dog his dinner in the car on a regular basis. Hand-feed your dog his dinner while he's in there. Give him stuffed **Kongs**® when he's in the car while you are at home and the car is parked. This process may take weeks to months, but it is a necessary accomplishment in order to bring your dog to the class. The last student I helped whose dog hated the car (she'd run away and hide in the house as soon as Lisa opened the garage door) had a dog who loved the car in less than a week!

Another option may be to drive your dog to the class, take a crate out of the car, and crate your dog next to the car. This way, the dog is still managed, but is not in a situation which will provoke a fear response. Of course, the crate will need to be situated so that the dog cannot see other dogs or people. And, of course, working with your dog on "liking the car" is still critical, since you must drive your dog to class and back! It is unrealistic for owners to think that they will never have to take their dog somewhere in a car.

You may be reading this and feeling great concern for all of these dogs in their cars in sweltering heat, freezing cold, or other weather hazards. I understand that conditions vary in different parts of the country; we were concerned about heat when I did a seminar in Phoenix, but on that day it was actually windy and cold! We had a large enough space inside in which to work the demo dogs; we chose to be away from the cold, rather than away from the heat! Silliness aside, this is no laughing matter. Dogs can become overheated easily in cars, and they can become too cold as well. Here are a few guidelines we use for our class:

In the heat: Find shade or make shade. Use the lightest material possible if you need to cover the car. Use a clip-on fan in the car. Open windows as much as possible while keeping your dog safely contained (another reason why crates are so wonderful). Wet his underside and legs. Offer water frequently. Apply a cold-wrap to his neck or a wet t-shirt to his body. When in doubt, check on the dog often and feed him for being quiet. Leave your car running with the air conditioning on if you feel you need to, even if for brief periods of time. The dogs come out of their cars often, so they are not locked in their cars for two hours at a time.

Here at Great Companions, we have a pond for the dogs to cool off in and sometimes we use it as part of the training! We will have two dogs walking around the pond, a distance apart from each other. In these cases, the dogs may be on a **longline** and they may choose to take themselves for a dip. This is fine, as long as the dog is checking in with his person! We also, on occasion, will get all of the dogs out of their cars at the same time and have them all work on focusing on their people. It is the owner's responsibility to put her dog back in her car and **have a party** for work well done before the dog becomes overstimulated and reacts. After the party, the dog comes out again and works some more. And, of course, if the dog reacts, the dog goes back into the car for a short period of time. This way, everyone gets more time out of the car, more time to work on their own, and the number of distractions is increased and variable.

We do have days when the heat index is predicted to be over 100° F. I will not hesitate to cancel class if we feel that the weather is too hot or too humid. The safety of the dogs is of paramount importance.

In the cold: Bundle up. Keep only one window open a crack. Use warm blankets over the cars and bedding in the crates. Have your dog wear a coat. If possible, park out of the wind. Check on the dog often and feed him for being quiet. Occasionally run the car with the heat on. I have one student who brings her husband and their other, nonreactive dog, and they hang out in the car together with the reactive dog! This way, they know that their dog's body temperature is comfortable. Again, the dogs come out of their cars frequently, so they will not be left in the cars unattended for long periods of time.

We do have days when the wind chill falls below 20° F. On these days, I do not hesitate to cancel class if we feel that the weather is too cold. We also do not work if there is inclement weather.

I feel strongly that it is more important for my students to survive than to get killed trying to come to class. If I am not sure what to do, I take a poll on our Yahoo! group. If the majority wants to cancel, we cancel. If the majority wants to have class but one or two people don't feel comfortable, then they don't come to class that night and they make it up. But expecting someone to come to class when he doesn't want to drive in ice or is worried about thunderstorms, for example, is counterproductive. These folks will arrive at class in an aroused state, the dogs sense it, and both the human's and the dog's work that night will suffer. Not a good choice.

In short, the use of the car is a great tool for running a reactive dog class. It has its benefits and its limitations, but the car can be a very flexible commodity. In addition, the car is a great way to take your teaching on the road during the week between classes. If you are not in a reactive dog class, you can use your car to take yourself and your dog to the distractions, rather than waiting for them to come to you! (See the "Flying Solo" chapter toward the end of this book.)

Smorgasbord

You will notice that we make liberal use of treats in our classes. Food and treats are a major focus of discussion at times; we share our treats with each other, talk about ingredients and sources of good treats, some of us make our own treats, and others of us actually taste the treats we give to our dogs! Why are we so crazy about treats?

We use food as a barometer for our dogs' emotional states. If the dog isn't taking treats, it's most likely because he is over-aroused or anxious. If a dog is not taking treats, his arousal level is such that he is not likely to learn anything. So if the dog isn't taking treats, it tells us that we need to back off the pressure, go more slowly, go farther away from the scary stimulus, or sometimes, use a better treat.

Food is an example of a **primary reinforcer**. This is something that's necessary for survival. Other examples of primary reinforcers are air, water, safety/shelter and sex. While some of these other things can be used (and indeed have been used with horses and zoo animals), there are ethical limitations. Food is simply the easiest to use because it's something we can easily add to the dog's existence. Most of the others need to be withheld and then provided as a reward; food can simply be added to what they get. Having said that, I often will instruct my students to feed less dinner or breakfast prior to working the dog in order to increase his attraction to the food. Rewarding with food also permits us to do rapid repetitions of new behaviors that we are teaching, thus accelerating the learning.

The complement to a primary reinforcer is a **secondary reinforcer**. These are things that are not necessary for survival, but through repeated association with a primary reinforcer become a conditioned reinforcer. Examples of this are verbal praise, petting or touching, and play. It has been said that anything can become a secondary reinforcer if it is paired enough times with a primary reinforcer. The **clicker** is really a secondary or conditioned reinforcer. It is important to understand that while you may think that petting your dog on the head is a good thing, he may not like it. Many dogs revile being petted. If your dog ducks his head or backs away, it's not a reward! Make sure you explore your dog's touching preferences. Acacia likes to be scratched under the chin, so I often use that. Verbal praise is also not necessarily rewarding to your dog, so it is important to frequently pair verbal praise with a primary reinforcer. While many dogs are toy fanatics, some dogs aren't very toy motivated, so this may or may not be a good option to use.

Once you have found a secondary reinforcer your dog loves, you can use it as a reward. Make certain that you pair it with primary reinforcers more often than not in order to maintain the value of the reward. Also, consider carefully the context in which you are using a secondary reinforcer. Many dogs will play at home but want no part of a ball or toy elsewhere. Sometimes this is simply a lack of generalization: he has only played ball in one or two particular places and believes that this is where they are to be played. Other times, the dog may be telling you that a particular reward is the only thing he's interested in. Offering him something he doesn't want as a reward is not rewarding! Remember, when we talk about rewards, it's what the *dog* finds rewarding, not what *you* think should be rewarding for him! This is a particularly critical concept when working with your reactive dog because we are working with a stressed dog, trying to maintain focus and keep him below the threshold of tolerance.

Now that you have read a primer on reinforcers, you can see that we use both primary and secondary reinforcers consistently. We use the clicker (secondary reinforcer), treats (primary reinforcers) and praise (secondary reinforcer) most of the time. Sometimes we'll use petting and toys, depending on the dog and the situation. But food ties everything together – it's the primary reinforcer.

For the most part, dogs much prefer meat over other types of food. On occasion, I see dogs in regular classes who love baby carrots or cheerios, but when we are working in high distraction environments, meaty is best. The treat should be smelly, which more often than not means it should be moist. Use fresh liver over freeze-dried liver in these situations. Use cheese over cheese-flavored dog treats. For a long time, I called Don "The Meatball Man" because he always had a large supply of meatballs for Mollie. We are all sure that Deb is known by the other dogs as "The Chicken Lady" because she almost always has freshly cooked chicken with her. We have also used steak, hot dogs, deli turkey, string cheese, smoked cheese, salami, and liverwurst. I admit that I always have a supply of Natural Balance® treats which I cut up before class. It has other ingredients, but its main ingredient is meat, and dogs love it. Peanut butter is also a great option; although not meat, it sure is smelly!

"Meaty" is the most important criteria for treats in my opinion, but there are other criteria which bear mentioning. I try very hard to avoid artificial colors and flavors; grains in general, but corn, wheat and soy in particular; artificial preservatives and fractionated proteins and grains. As a result, most commercially prepared dog treats are not on my list of favorites. This is not a requirement of my students, but it is something we often discuss.

The best option for using treats is to use a smorgasbord. Either have separate containers of different treats which you switch out to avoid boredom with the same old thing, or mix them all together so the dog never knows what he's going to get. The benefit to having separate containers is that you can save a really fabulous treat for an extremely high distraction situation or for a job spectacularly well done. And when you are in a class like mine, the dogs really get to sample a variety of yummy stuff!

It bears saying that we don't have hippopotami for dogs! Most of us don't feed our dogs their dinners if they are going to be coming to class in the evening. Some of us do bring some kibble to use for low level treats to round out the meal. We also try to use the smallest sized treat possible for the job. Occasionally, we need to use a larger treat so the dog can see it. This becomes necessary if the activity we are doing requires the tossing of food. We also pay attention to the color of the treat. Since dogs see purply-blues and orangy-yellows but not red or green, it's a hardship on a dog to have to quickly find a brown treat in grass, both of which probably appear as shades of gray to him. Instead, we'll use yellow or white cheese or chicken in grass. Finally, we notice the "tossability" of the treat. We often will toss treats to a dog as a part of an activity, usually classical conditioning. If a treat bounces and rolls too much, it can be stimulating or frustrating for the dog and potentially worrisome for the person because we are trying to keep a particular distance from the dog. So using a treat which isn't round can help.

In general, treats are a critical part of the work we do with reactive dogs. Knowing what your dog likes and dislikes, and when, is a vital part of the process. Recognizing that a treat no longer holds particular value for your dog is also important.

Thinking on Your Feet

The challenge to setting up a class for reactive dogs, or to working with one's own reactive dog, is that the variables which can be worked are endless. I have no predetermined syllabus for class; it is ongoing and individualized. A student doesn't just join on week one and follow the homework sheets and progress through the class like they would for my basic obedience ("Foundations") class. Each dog has his own triggers, stress level and needs. And so do the owners! Some dogs are reactive to just people, some to just dogs, some to people and dogs, some to sounds, some to smells, and some to everything! And since reactivity can have origins in genetics, environment, trauma or socialization, there are too many factors to consider in training and treatment to standardize it.

Working with a reactive dog is a long-term and sometimes painfully slow process. In light of this challenge, I have set forth to outline some of the myriad activities that we have done in our reactive classes with different dogs. I decided to log a sequence of weeks in our class. The entry for each week includes a description of the activities for each participating dog, along with any discussions that pertained to the dog or the activity. Sometimes, progress is immediately obvious and exciting. Sometimes it seems that for weeks on end a dog works on the same issue, at the same level, and makes little or no progress. Sometimes we make mistakes and have to backtrack. Once in a while, we have to guess and feel our way through a problem to find a solution. It's all documented here, and you can see progress that is palpable.

It is my hope that by laying down these exercises and activities, they will be of assistance to others who are trying to help reactive dogs. For the most part, there is no particular order for the exercises. Sometimes a student wants to work on one aspect of reactivity one week and a different aspect the next week. If there is a skill prerequisite for an activity, it will be mentioned the first time that activity is outlined. Associated terminology will also be outlined, shown in bold text the first time it is used, and defined (see the "Glossary").

You will notice that the students in the class take responsibility for setting their own goals and deciding what they want to work on. This class also serves very much as a support group. During the week, we all communicate by means of an online discussion (Yahoo!) group which was formed just for the class. We ask each other questions, update each other on progress and frustrations, and decide what we want to work on during class. It wasn't always this way; for a long time, we would start each class with a **pow-wow**. We would sit around and recount how each dog's week was, what we wanted to work on, and sometimes we'd discuss new concepts or I would teach a new skill. But we found that this required a significant portion of our time (usually 45 to 60 minutes), and that meant that our dogs were anxiously awaiting us. Since some of the dogs had some separation anxiety issues, we changed the format. The online forum is very helpful, and we are still able to discuss issues in person during class time if we need to do so. While I am the instructor of the class, I encourage my students to think for themselves. This often pays off! Many minds together can come up with much better ideas than one mind. Besides, my students know their dogs much better than I do, so it makes sense to encourage them to figure out how to rehabilitate their own dogs, with my guidance and the support of the group. Since they will be with their dogs for the rest of the dogs' lives, they will need to know what to do and how to do it without relying on someone else. Not only am I teaching the dogs to be thinking creatures, I am also teaching the human end of the leash.

Toward the end of the book, you'll find a glossary of terms I've used in the discussions. The concepts of these terms are very important to remember and to utilize with your reactive dog or in your reactive dog class.

Because we will be following the progress of the dogs who have attended the class repeatedly over a period of time, you'll want to know something about them. Without further ado, let's meet the dogs!

Cast of Characters

It's time to meet the players in this book. They run the full gamut; young and old, male and female, spayed or neutered and intact, purebred and mix, rescues and purchased dogs. As you will see, reactivity doesn't affect just one part of dogdom. Each biography is written by the dog's owner.

MOLLIE

Kim, Don and DJ

Mollie is a four-year-old spayed Border Collie. We got her at about age
4½ months from a kennel that sold many breeds (pure and mixed) of puppies.
She was shy and fearful when we brought her home. She did get used to her
new surroundings, but anything that was new or scary would send her hiding,
barking, or to the point of shutting down. In addition to Mollie, we also have
a lizard. Mollie doesn't pay any attention to her at all. She does, however,
absolutely love one of my mom's cockatiels. She will spend hours watching
him and he does the same with her. They have a weird relationship!

I can't really think of anything in particular that initiated her reactive
behavior; I think she was kept too long at the kennel. Environmental, human
and other animal exposure seemed to be limited. She didn't seem to know
what grass was, was shy of people, and when we brought in to our home,
she crawled into the bottom shelf of the bookcase and just laid there, visibly
frightened.

We didn't take Mollie for any formal training when we got her, but I did
work with her on my own, and my son's girlfriend helped with some things.
She had some experience working with pups being trained as future service
dogs. Mollie learned a couple of basic commands (sit, down, give paw, high
five).

When I started the reactive classes at Great Companions, I absolutely loved
it. I had never used clicker training before. It was a huge help with working
with Mollie. I have to admit I had a LOT to learn about myself before I could
really begin to help Mollie. Simple things – like the way I was standing, how
I was reacting to her behaviors, etc. Mollie was quick to shut down whenever
she was uncomfortable or confused by anything so we had to take it really
slow. It was probably a few months before we got her to focus on me instead of
distractions. We did a lot of **stuff-a-dogs** in the beginning. I can remember in
the beginning during our private lessons, she would only do so much and then
she would want to hide under the table or curl up in a corner somewhere. We
have been attending the reactive dog classes for nearly three years.

When I think back on what we've learned during that time, I don't even
know where to begin! There is a huge difference in so many different ways.
She once would cower away from people or try to run and hide if people would
try to approach or pet her. She had to make the first move toward allowing you
into her circle of friends. She is more relaxed with people now, though she
still prefers to be the one approaching or making the first move. Thinking back,
there were times when all someone had to do was take a step or two toward

her and she would lose it, barking and trying to run away to avoid them. She's definitely gained some confidence, too, and doesn't shut down nearly as often. I've learned to watch her "signs" of stress and do something about them now instead of allowing her to get to the point of shutting down. I think she has learned to check in with us more instead of just letting her fears take over. But, to us, it's not just about what's changed in Mollie through this process but how we have changed as a team because I think I've learned so much as well. I've learned how to get focus, how not to reward behaviors I don't want, and how to read and pay more attention to Mollie. I know I am a lot different from that person who started the lessons with no clue about training and fumbling with clicker and treats. It is a miracle that Mollie learned anything back then.

Mollie decided that she didn't like the clicker after about two years of training her with it. There was no one event that made her sensitive to it, and it took us a while to figure it out. We just switched to a **verbal marker** instead, and she is fine with that.

I love the classes and strongly believe in Ali's method of training. I guess the only thing that we could improve on is our long-windedness at times because it can cut into our work time, but we've gotten a lot better at that too. Knowing that we've all become sort of support group for each other makes the classes even better. Being able to share good and bad experiences, sharing ideas on training and changing behaviors, comparing the types of treats we use and much more, all make the classes much more special.

BAILEY

Kristen (and Linda)

My best guess is that Bailey is a Labrador retriever/Shar Pci mix and about 5½ years old. I had him neutered when I got him, when he was about three years old. I got him from the Delaware County SPCA. At first, I was just fostering him. However, after his reactivity began, it became clear that he was unadoptable. I chose to keep him and work with him rather then recommend that he be put down.

His separation anxiety became apparent almost immediately. The day I brought him home, I went out to buy him some things. I had a large crate for him, so I put him in it. He had a panic attack and somehow bent the bars and squeezed out underneath.

I had a hard time leaving the house; he would block the door with his body and not allow me to shut the door. I worked with him using desensitization techniques and a **Kong®**. Slowly he became better at me leaving. My vet also prescribed **Clomicalm®** (an anti-anxiety medication) for him for awhile. When I started the reactivity class, I was unable to leave him alone in my car. My mother sat with him for many weeks until we felt that we could leave him alone in the car. Even then he was very anxious, and I worked on this by treating him for not whining. He is now to the point where I can leave him alone in the car during class, although he sometimes has a setback.

Bailey reacts to unfamiliar people and dogs, particularly if they're moving. Joggers are especially difficult for him. Before, it seemed that on walks if the person had a dog with him, it was easier for Bailey. I wonder if it's possible that his reactivity is more him wanting to interact but is not sure how to do that. I'm sure that some of his reactivity is also frustration. If he sees a dog at home, either through the window or in the front yard, he is definitely reactive. Perhaps that has something to do with territoriality. He is generally fine with noises unless they are associated with people such as a doorbell, knock, or car door slamming out front.

Bailey began reacting to things within the first couple of months that I had him, but I suspect that he was reactive before I got him. There seemed to be no one event that started him on the path to reactivity, at least not since I've had him. He had been abused in his previous home; he has two floating ribs that were broken and never healed properly. He had been abandoned in his home after his family moved away and left him. He is now a lean and healthy 70 lbs. When I took him home, he was only 50 lbs, with a poor quality, very brittle coat; now, it shines and looks very healthy. Feeding him a raw diet has certainly helped, as has stabilizing his hypothyroidism with medications.

Bailey and I live with three cats. He has a very high prey drive, and this causes problems. He has trouble controlling the urge to chase them. Ironically, at the shelter when he was "cat tested," he showed ZERO interest in the cat. I guess he just wanted outta there! He does distinguish between "his" cats and others and is willing to not chase my mom's cats when outdoors at her house. He is content to chase the ball and will ignore her cat when she runs. Neighborhood cats are fair game in his mind, though.

Soon after I got Bailey, my aunt started me with a **counter conditioning** program using the clicker, while I found a local positive trainer. I worked with that trainer for a little while at home. We thought that he was ready for a small-group class (as a stepping stone to entry to a local canine sports facility) and that's what led me to Great Companions. We took *Foundations* and *Beyond the Basics* in a daytime class of three in the fall of 2004, then began reactive dog class in February 2005. Back then we walked more in public, but he would react all the time.

Once we started the reactive class, progress with Bailey was excruciatingly slow. It took him weeks to be able to even get out of the car without barking. It was comforting to see others in similar situations though; it's a very therapeutic environment – much like AA. It's taken Bailey a long time to learn to focus on me over the reactive stimuli; he still has trouble! But he is doing much better now. As recently as a year ago, Bailey would react (bark) if he caught someone making eye contact with him. Now, he looks forward to coming to class and seeing all the people! He happily goes up to people to get treats. He will sit for them and do other simple tricks. Recently, there was a new couple there, people he had never seen before, and he took food from them!! This was huge for Bailey – he has come so far. It is still difficult for him; you can read it in his body language, so we keep these intense sessions short. But he really wants to see the people. He really does like people, and because of this class, we have been able to help him work through his fears with strangers. We've been attending the class for just about two years now.

Bailey is a very different dog now, much more relaxed, even just at home. I can introduce new people into his life (if done properly) – both male and female – and he accepts them! I've even had small groups of people over to the house. Walking with him is much less stressful, although I need to work on MY stress levels and my courage to challenge him more. I still can't really take him places other than the park-like setting of the hospital near my home. His car behavior is better; he now only reacts to people at close range. He still barks out the front window at people and noises and at the mailman. In general, I can't think of any way in which Bailey's behavior has deteriorated since we started the reactive class.

If I had to find something about the reactive class that is a problem, I'd say that we all need to remember to chit-chat online rather than in class; especially when there are more dogs in class (attendance can vary from four to seven dogs). It is too easy to start talking and that takes up working time for the dogs. That being said – it is well worth the hour drive each week!

MAGGIE

Colleen and Tracy

Maggie came to us from a friend who bred her. We got her when she was 11 months old. She was sold as a puppy to a family with a young child. Apparently, there was an "incident" with the young child (who I believe was about seven at the time), in which the child told his parents that Maggie had bitten him. There were no marks on him and no one saw anything, so no one knows for sure, but the parents decided to turn Maggie over to the SPCA where she was quarantined for ten days, and then she was returned to the breeder. She knew that my husband and I had just moved to our farm and we were looking for a dog and we had no children. So, we took Maggie.

We discovered very early on that Maggie has a serious issue with hands and being touched anywhere on her body, particularly around her head. Although Maggie has come very far with Tracy and me, we are always careful when we expose her to something new. She doesn't like strangers or children. You can really see it in her eyes. When she is uncomfortable with something or someone, she shows **whale eye**, and the next thing she will do is snap. This frightened me initially because I believed she was trying to bite. That is when I called Great Companions for help. I was relieved to learn that if Maggie really wanted to bite, she would. Her snap is a warning to back off because she is scared. I will never know the full extent of what caused her to be this way, but it is something that we have learned to manage through training. It will never be completely gone, but we have reached a point where we know how to manage her and develop trust with her. She is very particular about strangers. There are certain people she is instantly comfortable with and some people that she is never comfortable around. She does not like children or small, short people (that look like children). Her hackles go up, she growls, and I cannot trust her around strangers. If someone exhibits the slightest bit of fear around her, she becomes very worried and reactive.

We have another Boxer named Milton. Milton recently graduated from *Foundations* at Great Companions with flying colors. He does not have the kind of issues Maggie has. The two get along very well and play together for hours. Maggie has always been very good with other dogs. We also have a house cat that Maggie and Milton occasionally chase around the house, but no problems there. We have a barn full of horses and Maggie knows to stay clear of them.

I really enjoyed the reactive class a lot. I learned a lot. I had never had a dog before that needed that kind of training and I was really at a loss. I just didn't know where to start and I was worrying about liability issues with a dog who had a propensity to snap. The use of the treat/clicker showed immediate results with getting Maggie to focus. The other people in the class were extremely supportive, which helped, too. The first day there I thought, "Oh, my gosh, everyone will think my dog is so mean and evil!" But in reality, all the dogs had issues and each one was different but equally frustrating to their respective humans. Everyone in the class obviously loved their dogs and wanted to improve the quality of their lives with their dogs to best of their ability, which I found inspiring and motivating. I started the reactive class with private sessions in the spring of 2006 and continued through that summer.

I believe Maggie has improved tremendously. She will never be a dog we can leave alone with strangers and never around any children. We have learned how to manage her, and Tracy and I are able to handle her because she trusts us. She knows that Tracy and I aren't going to hurt her and she has learned how to enjoy being touched and handled instead of always scared, protective of herself, and "reactive."

One of the most valuable things I learned from my experience with Maggie is that everyone who owns a dog, regardless of how well-behaved they are or whatever issues they have, needs to enroll in, at the very least, one good quality basic class on obedience. There are little things that can be done from the very beginning that will have a lasting effect on the dog. A well-disciplined dog is a happy dog...I really believe that. I believe there are too many people that get into dog ownership without taking the time to teach the dog basic skills that ultimately save his life some day. Calling him back should he run into the street, teaching him to "leave it," teaching them to "stay," getting the dog focused on you, proper leash walking. I never realized how important they were until we got Maggie.

SPENCER

Laura

Spencer Michael is a Rottweiler/German Shepherd mix, about four years old, and neutered. When he was 16½ months old, I got Spencer from an acquaintance that was moving and was unsuccessful at finding him a home. For the first couple of months, his owners kept him tied to a pole 24/7 to "make him a guard dog," and the kids in the neighborhood tormented him "for fun." His second owner rescued him to get him out of that situation and she had him for only a few weeks. His third owner, who never owned a dog before, worked two jobs, and Spencer spent most of his time (18 hours a day) in his crate. I adopted him in March of 2004.

Spencer reacts to just about anything and everything that's unfamiliar to him. He had been reacting since I rescued him. I didn't even know what "reacting" was then until I met Ali. When I first adopted Spencer, my ex had a Boston terrier and a hound/shepherd mix. They got along well. I remember the first night I brought Spencer home; he was actually scared to enter my house because the Boston terrier was standing by the door. Spencer cowered and sat down on the porch and refused to go in my house, the house alarm was going off, the police ended up coming, it was a mess, I had to put Spencer in the car and isolate the other dogs so I could get Spencer inside. After the initial sniffing, everything was fine. A year-and-a-half later, I moved in with my Aunt, and she has a Weimaraner. Her dog is a lot more passive than Spencer; they get along for the most part except when Spencer tries to get her to play with him.

Shortly after I got him, Spencer and I went to group obedience classes for several months off and on and he also went to a three-day overnight doggie boot camp. We used choke chains and went over basic commands in the middle of a big pet food store on Saturday morning. Let's just say that Spencer and I got kicked out of class more times than we actually were in class!

When I started classes at Great Companions, I found that the class set us up to succeed. That was great! Spencer is like the kid that gets picked last in gym class. Reactive class was great for his ego (or shall I say my self-esteem!). It's a great support group. I didn't think Spencer would ever be able to do anything in class. I though that he'd react to everyone all the time. I even used two leashes on him, one on his harness and one on his collar, just for safety. I was really afraid to bring him out of the car the first few times! But when I did, I was really surprised! Just the distance from the other stimuli seemed to help him be able to focus on me almost immediately and consistently. After a while, no one believed me that Spencer was reactive!

Spencer and I attended the reactive classes for about ten months, until my work schedule changed and I was unable to make it to classes any more. But we learned a lot during the classes and I know how to handle him better now. He is less reactive to the neighbor's dog as well as the neighbor, and I find that I can walk him in more places than I used to be able to go. We also use the long line now, which helps Spencer to get better exercise. Spencer is a big dog!

ELVIS

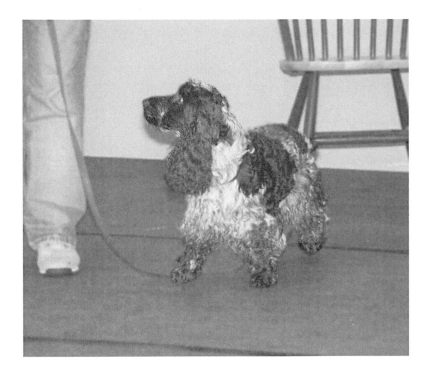

Deb

I got Elvis after I had given up trying to convince my Lowchen, Mickey, to really enjoy agility. I had looked at several different breeds, settling on Cocker Spaniels. I talked to a few different breeders and then a friend of mine steered me to a breeder of English Cocker Spaniels that someone she knew had bought from twice before.

The first time I called, the breeder told me she didn't have any puppies available, but she invited me to come down to a hunt test they were having

45 minutes from my home. I liked what I saw and spoke with several people there. The dogs and people in the club were all friendly and outgoing. The dogs were energetic but not manic. Some of the people I talked with also did agility training and were pleased with their progress. A couple of weeks later, the breeder called and told me that she might, indeed, have a puppy available from her current litter, which was about ten weeks old then. The breeder only raises one or two litters a year and generally had five or six dogs in her house at any one time. She raises the puppies in the house; before their first shots, they are kept in a separate room but as they got older were kept in a play pen in the middle of the family room. The puppies were partially house trained, handled regularly but not to excess.

I went down once to visit the puppies and did a simple temperament test to evaluate personality and confidence. The puppy who would eventually become "Elvis" passed easily. He was friendly and playful and would allow himself to be placed on his back and have his paws touched. I felt like he would be a good choice.

Although Elvis was a little smaller than the other puppies, he had a beautiful head and the most adorable dark blue roan paws, hence his registered name of "Blue Suede Shoes." We picked him up two weeks later when he was about 14 weeks old. Since he did have promise from a conformation standpoint, I committed to not neuter him and at least try to get his championship.

Our first challenge was to get Elvis and Mickey used to one another. Mickey was over three and used to being the only dog in the house. Elvis had typical puppy enthusiasm and had a tendency to play rough. We made a point of putting Elvis in his place: we fed Mickey first, kept Elvis in the crate for periods during the day to give Mickey a break, and didn't let Elvis ever sleep in our bed.

We started taking Elvis to puppy classes within two months. We also took him to beginning obedience classes. Elvis always seemed relaxed in class. He didn't seem afraid of the other dogs, nor did he seem especially interested in them. As the weather got warmer, I started to take him to agility class with Mickey, just to socialize. Again he got lots of attention and didn't seem to have a problem with any of the other dogs. During his first summer, we took a break from obedience classes, but I continued to take him to agility and to start getting him used to some of the equipment. He had an extremely short attention span, but I continued to just spend breaks working him between runs with Mickey.

In the fall, after Elvis was a year old, I started to focus on his training. Our biggest difficulty originally was trying to keep him focused on agility rather than the other dogs and people. As soon as he got off lead he would run up to the other dogs he saw. He wasn't aggressive, just wanted to play or even just sniff all the interesting smells that are common in a riding ring; however, it was not acceptable behavior and we weren't making any progress. So I started training him on a long line. This worked pretty well for a while. Whenever he lost focus and began to run off, I'd step on the rope and get his attention. Training started to go well, he loved the equipment, was very fast when focused and I was feeling good about his prospects.

At the same time we started to go to handling classes and occasional conformation matches. He was a squirmer and a sniffer and so he didn't show well as an adolescent, but we didn't have any issues with other dogs or people.

The first time I noticed anything reactive about Elvis was in conformation handling class when he was about 18 months old. He barked and growled at a boxer in the class. I don't think the boxer did anything to provoke it, certainly nothing I could see. One of the trainers recommended sternly reprimanding him and spraying him in the face with water. Another trainer mentioned that I was not keeping him focused enough. I started bringing tons of treats and not feeding him prior to class, which worked 90% of the time, but if he happened to look a dog in the eye, there was a strong possibility he would react.

Around the same time, I sent him out with a professional handler a couple of times. The handler, who also showed Bouviers, said he was good with the other English cockers, but had a real hard time with the Bouviers. Also I noticed that at agility class he started reacting badly to some Siberian huskies as well as boxers that were regular attendees. Suddenly I had a dog that was unpredictable with other dogs. He also started barking at certain people as well.

The low point came soon after his second birthday. First, he growled at some other dogs and maybe even one of the other people at handling class. The next week he lunged and growled at a Siberian who surprised us at agility and the trainer subsequently asked me not to return until he was under control. I was devastated. Suddenly I couldn't do the very thing I had gotten him for. Should I have him neutered? Were there other alternatives? I knew the problem was bigger than I could handle. I needed to get professional help.

YANKEE

Marie and Mark

We cannot remember exactly why we starting looking for a second dog. Our "old girl" Layla, a 12-year-old female chocolate lab, was having good and bad days with her health and mobility. Maybe we were afraid of being "dog-less" if she died. Maybe it was an unsolicited email or link from a dog-related web site. Regardless of the path, we found ourselves meeting Yankee one day in July. Yankee came to us from an online rescue group. His online personal ad showed a sorrowful 75 lb male Golden Retriever - Yellow Lab mix, about seven years old with a scar on his nose. He had the typical hard-luck story; two or three past owners that for one reason or another had to give him up, and then some time on his own running loose.

The first introductory meeting at our house went wonderfully. He was a shy, quiet dog. His only desire was to be petted. Continuously. Yankee and Layla met in our yard and got along well. We decided to adopt this healthy, seemingly well-behaved dog. We decided Yankee needed formal training so we took him to Ali's *Foundations* class. During the first several classes, Yankee was attentive and did not interact with the younger dogs during play-time. We always walk Yankee on a leash. He was okay when walking in the neighborhood or in the park where we occasionally saw dogs and horses. He did pull on the leash, but did not react.

Then he changed...

After three or four *Foundations* classes, he began to bark at the other dogs and behave badly. We had to remove him from the training area to a place where he could not see the other dogs. We tried this several times and his behavior gradually deteriorated with more barking. His behavior when walking at the park also worsened. He would bark and pull anytime he saw another dog. He would act like a nut-case.

In the car, he is nervous and cannot relax. In the beginning he would not sit or lay down in the back seat. With training, he now lays down for short periods. When riding in the car, he will bark at people walking or riding bikes, dogs and other animals (squirrels, horses, etc.). The duration and intensity of this barking has decreased as we work with Yankee. But this is based on the proximity of the person or animal to the car. The closer the object, the louder and longer the duration of his barking.

Yankee is terrified of thunderstorms, fireworks, and blowing across the top of a bottle. He seems to be able to sense the approach of a thunderstorm. He becomes panicky and beings to frantically pace and drool. He tries to find a place to hide, but won't settle in one place. We tried setting up a hidey-hole, using a flexible crate and blankets. He wanted no part of that. During one storm when we were not home, he severely damaged molding around a door and drywall as he tried to get into the garage, seemingly, to find a place to hide. After trying several techniques to get him over storms, we found the **Storm Defender cape**™. This reduced his storm anxiety to a point that is manageable. Now he likes to hide in the bedroom closet during storms.

MAX

Patti, Glen and Tara

My husband Glen, my daughter Tara and I live with Max, who entered our lives in December 2005 when he was approximately nine weeks of age. We adopted him from a local shelter that provided little information regarding his early days except to say that he had been rescued from a shelter in Ohio that planned to destroy him. The adoption papers described him as a black lab mix, which was two-thirds correct. He is black (except for a few white markings) and he is a mix, although probably not lab. Everyone's best guess is that he is part Border collie. The only other information we were given by the shelter was that he was a male (we're sure they were right about that) and that he had been neutered (we hope they were right about that!).

When we first brought him home, he was somewhat timid, but he seemed to adjust well to our family and the vet told us that he appeared healthy. The biggest thing we noticed when we first got him was how much different he was from our first dog, Grinch, around food. Whereas Grinch practically inhaled anything edible, Max ate very slowly and was reluctant to taste new things. He definitely was not outgoing with people, but we did not notice him being particularly fearful at first.

When he was five months old we enrolled him in a puppy training class at a local pet store. A big part of the class dealt with housetraining and other behavioral issues. We also spent time learning simple commands such as "sit," "down," "stay," and "wait." Max learned quickly, and because he was "calmer" than many of the other puppies the instructor often used him to demonstrate various training techniques to the group. In later weeks, the instructor started having us work with the dogs out in the store and this is when we first noticed a problem with Max. He started to try and run away whenever people approached him in the aisles. Some weeks we just opted to stay in the training room with him and work on things there. At the last class, the instructor brought in a tunnel for a "fun" activity. One by one all the other puppies went happily through. Then came Max's turn. He wanted no part of it. We tried luring him with treats, other dogs, and getting in the tunnel ourselves. In the end, we sort of shoved him through.

I am not sure if the tunnel incident was to blame, but by the time we took him back to the pet store a couple of months later for the intermediate class, his fearfulness had heightened considerably. Not only was he uncomfortable being out in the store, but he started to withdraw from people in the classroom, hiding in the corner and/or under the chairs. Every week as the other dogs and owners would head out into the store, the instructor would say, "I'll come back to help you guys in a little bit." But she never did. By the time the class concluded, we felt embarrassed, bewildered and discouraged by his behavior.

Not sure what to do next, my husband went on the internet and searched for information regarding fearfulness in dogs. This search provided a link to Ali's website which provided a description of "reactive" dogs and the work that she does with them. Max seemed to fit into this category and so we called the next day to enroll him in the class. When we first started in the reactive class it was all very new to me and a little overwhelming. I was somewhat discouraged by the fact that Max seemed to be so far behind the other dogs in the group. I also felt as if the other members of the group spent so much of their time and effort (and treats) trying to help Max. I wanted to be able to reciprocate but because I was new the other dogs were not as familiar with me and so usually I couldn't participate in working with them. We've been attending the class for over six months now so I am more able to interact with the other dogs. As far as Max goes, I do still feel like he is so far behind the others in the group, but I can see that he is making progress. He will now approach people to take treats right out of their hand – something he NEVER would have done before. I have learned that progress comes in little steps and that it does not always occur in a straight line. There are now times and places where Max focuses pretty well. Yet there are still many instances where he is unable to focus on me when confronted with scary stimuli. Since joining the class the only way in which he has gotten worse, if you can call it that, is that he has become reactive to the clicker. I'm not really sure why – I think he is just very sound sensitive.

I feel so fortunate to have found this class. Everyone in the group has been so great in offering help and suggestions. I can not imagine a more caring, supportive group. There is nothing I would choose to change about it.

SHADOW

Christi and Pat

Shadow is a neutered Corgi mix. He is about five years old. My husband and I adopted him almost a year ago when he was about four from an animal rescue.

When we first brought Shadow home, he was the perfect gentleman; he would not even jump on the couch unless we invited him. Shadow and Betsy, our two-year-old German shepherd mix, have gotten along great from day one. Shadow puts up with all of Betsy's antics. Betsy always wants to play and even if Shadow is not in the mood, she pesters him until he finally gives in and plays with her without a bark or even a growl.

Betsy was kind of a "toy-hog" so my husband decided to take Shadow to the pet store after we had him about a week to get him his very own toy. Shadow seemed a little timid in the store, although he did not bark at anyone. We did find it a little peculiar that he would not take the treat that the cashier offered him, but we decided that he was still getting used to his new home and surroundings and maybe he had never been to the pet store before and did not know what to do.

For the first month when I took Shadow and Betsy for a walk together they were great. They love to go on walks and usually walk right next to each other. If either one of them got over-excited or out of hand, it was usually Betsy. We used to tease Betsy and tell her to be more like Shadow. Little did we know…

If we had to pinpoint one particular incident wherein Shadow started to become reactive, it may be that one day, soon after we got Shadow, my husband and I were walking the dogs. I had Betsy and he had Shadow. From across an open field, we could see two women walking their dogs off-leash. The dogs started running towards us. The dogs didn't seem to be vicious, but they weren't listening to their owners, either. The dogs ran over to our dogs and were just sniffing. Our dogs didn't seem to mind too much, but my husband and I were rather upset and worried as the two other dogs came running towards us. The women came over and finally took their dogs away (no apology offered). It's hard to say if this had a bearing on his behavior. We could have transferred our fear to him.

There was not a point where Shadow was walking along happily one day and then the next day was reactive. It happened very slowly, starting with other dogs and then with people. In the beginning we would think that he just didn't like a particular dog or person or he was having a bad day until it came to a point where we couldn't deny it any longer – he began barking and lunging at everyone.

Shadow and I first took three private classes with Ali. After the first class and a few days of practicing what she taught us, Shadow and I were on a walk and another person walked by. Shadow started his usual barking and lunging at the poor guy, but low and behold, when I called his name, he turned around to look at me. He only paused for a split second, but this was a huge breakthrough for him. He was always in his own world until the offending person or dog passed us. Now for the first time, he actually acknowledged that I was there too!

Since then it has been a slow but rewarding process. Shadow has had his setbacks, but has definitely continued to make progress.

Although I have been working with Shadow every day for the past four months with Ali's guidance, we have only been in the Reactive Class for a few weeks now. By the time I started the actual Reactive Class, Shadow had made such great strides that I was ready to try anything with Ali. Shadow can now walk into a room full of people plus another dog and pretend (for a little while) that I am the only person in the room. I can tell it is still a great effort for him to keep his attention on me. He is, of course, aware of the other people and dog, and will lose his focus if I am not 100% focused on him, but he is doing better than I ever thought possible.

Shadow does much better now when we are walking alone. He can usually ignore other people and most dogs as long as I am feeding him treats along the way. If he starts to bark or lunge, I can usually get his attention back without too much effort. However, when Betsy is with us, I think she senses the tension in Shadow and starts barking herself. She usually will bark first and this of course sets Shadow off and we're back to the barking and lunging showdown. It's not quite as bad as before and is something that we need to keep working on. By the way, Betsy has no reactivity problem when she is walked by herself and wants nothing more than to meet and greet every person and dog that we pass by.

The thing that I am most thrilled with since we started training with Ali is that Shadow seems like a much happier dog now. He is still a gentleman around the house, but will initiate play with Betsy as much as she does with him and if we're lucky, he will even play with us humans! I find that each day brings new challenges and opportunities for us to work and learn together so that Shadow can be the best dog he can be and I can be the best Mom I can be.

When Shadow first became reactive, we tried everything we could think of to get him to stop. Some things didn't work at all and some things worked for a while and then stopped working. With Ali Brown's instruction we know we are definitely on the right path this time and will continue to utilize her techniques.

INDY

Lisa

I received AfterAll's India Ink when she was nine weeks old from a breeder in Texas. She is one of six dogs I own, all Aussies. She was a very loving puppy and adored all who came near her until one day when she was about four months old, while watching an agility class a very bold poodle was allowed to approach her. He proceeded to go after her with snarling teeth. She ran and jumped on my lap and shook. Well...we can say that started her reactive behavior towards other dogs. Shortly after that, I took her to a dog show. She was lunging at all the dogs who walked by. I just thought she was being a brat until I took her for some introductory work in agility with Ali. We thought it would be great for her to play with Ali's Belgian Sheepdog, Bing, but she was very snarly and barky with him, even from a distance. The second time she saw him, he was across the pond, and she still had that reaction!

She is now 14 months old (still intact, as she is a show dog) and with the guidance of Ali, and the help of the reactive dog class, I can finally see the light at the end of the tunnel. I've learned to teach her to look to me for help instead of going after the other dogs immediately. She has progressed so well that she has gone to a few shows and actually enjoyed herself without coming unglued. It has certainly made our bond stronger. We still have work to do, but it is definitely a positive direction.

ACACIA

Ali Brown

I bought Acacia from a reputable breeder when she was nine weeks old. I had seen her several times before I brought her home. I was determined that she would be my completely-clicker trained dog; she has never seen a choke chain or a prong collar. Starting at about five months, she was a little leery of strangers, but we constantly worked through it, having strangers offer her treats. Acacia began her conformation career at age six months, and finished her championship title at age 13½ months.

By age two, I decided that I would have her spayed because I didn't want to breed her. Aside from the fact that I really didn't have the knowledge required to start breeding, I wasn't really happy with her standoffishness and her occasional reactive interactions with some dogs. As soon as I spayed her, she became "fat and aggressive." Her tendency toward suspicion of strangers increased until she became untrustworthy and she began preemptive attacks on dogs that she thought might offend her. Any time a person or dog suddenly appeared, Acacia would react. Dogs who came right up to her were cause for concern because sometimes they might jump on her. When she had altercations with people, it was of the "run up and growl" variety. When she went after dogs, she would often leave her trademark cut under the eye. On two occasions, she jumped up and nipped the sleeve of people. In both circumstances, they were preteens walking toward her (I believe this was an age group that I missed in socializing her), and in both circumstances, she deftly placed a small tooth hole in the material without touching the skin.

But that was enough; I realized that Acacia was a liability. Mortified that I was a dog trainer and had such a problem dog, I had to either euthanize her or fix her. I began my search for the cure. It quickly became apparent, through working with a trainer, that there was no "fixing" this problem. It was going to be a lifetime of management. Great. Just what I needed.

The methods outlined in *Scaredy Dog!* and in this book are the methods that I used with Acacia. I also began feeding her a raw diet and testing her thyroid on a yearly basis. Each year, the results would come back within normal limits. After the third year of this, as I watched my dog become fatter and fatter – despite feeding this 80 lb dog ¾ cup of kibble a day – I learned about the work of Dr. Jean Dodds (see "Resources and Reading"). I had my vet draw the blood and I sent it out to Hemopet myself. (My vet was not particularly supportive of this or my choice of feeding a raw diet, and I soon found one who is more open-minded.) The results came back…I was vindicated! Acacia's thyroid was low, and we started her immediately on supplements. I quickly saw a difference in her, although the weight loss continued to be a struggle. But one of the wonderful results was that I felt less guilty for what Acacia was experiencing, and now I could spend my energy on more positive things.

I have been very fortunate. Acacia got her Canine Good Citizen certificate, became a Therapy Dog, and has earned a long string of Rally-Obedience titles. She travels with me to do seminars on reactivity and is my demo dog for my classes. She has become the teacher. She teaches other dogs what to do. She is more mellow in her middle-aged years, but she is still reactive. While I do have to constantly manage her, it is such a habit now that we rarely even think about it. When we are careless, we are reminded!

One of Acacia's special talents is to focus on me and back up toward a dog. She trusts me enough to follow my cues. Together, we teach reactive dogs how to "sniff butts" to learn about other dogs without the threat. It is a very special skill and I feel very lucky to have developed this level of trust with her. What a great dog!

The Classes

The ensuing pages provide a detailed description of the weekly classes I've conducted at Great Companions over a period of eight months. A few students leave and a few new ones join, and the exercises change from week to week, but the intent of this "project" for me is to share with the reader many of the techniques that we use in the class. I tried to provide as much detail as possible about the activities, the owners' responses, the dogs' responses, the mistakes we made, and the successes we achieved.

It's very easy to make mistakes in this type of setting because the trainer and the owners are always thinking on their feet. Even after we changed the protocol and class format from the pow-wow to the online planning discussion, we sometimes made changes at the last moment. The reasons are many: a dog might not be feeling well, it might have been too warm or too cold to do what was planned, a dog may have reacted at a higher level to a stimulus than we thought he would so we had to make the next exercise simpler, unplanned-for distractions may have created a more difficult situation than anticipated, etc. Occasionally, a dog's response to a set of stimuli is so good that we prolong the session or alter it to allow for more work to be done at that time, or to increase the amount of distraction or stimulation. While there is much science in this approach, there is also much art. I often will change my mind at the last moment. Sometimes I wonder why I did it or a student may ask me why, and it's often a gut reaction. Happily, though, my students almost always know why I did what I did without me having to explain it!

Some of these students were relatively new to the class, while others have been coming to these classes for a year or more. You will be seeing a glimpse of the dogs' progress; some of these dogs have made astonishing gains, while others are about to make great changes. The descriptions below are not intended to be a full biography of the rehabilitation of the dogs, but rather, a running dialogue which outlines suggestions for activities which can be done in other reactive classes or on your own if you have no reactive class nearby. Overall, though, you will see how each dog changes and learns over time. You should be seeing trends in their behavior changes, with small downturns in their learning. Nothing was left out. The successes and failures are all there, as are the brilliant moments and the huge trainer errors.

The format of these reactive classes allows for socialization on the part of the humans as well as re-socialization for the dogs. Together, we learn a little bit about each other and a lot about our dogs.

July Twentieth

Present: Kim, Don and Mollie; Marie, Mark and Yankee; Laura and Spencer; Kristen, Linda and Bailey; Colleen, Tracy and Maggie.

Tonight we decided to start with a shorter discussion so that we could work the dogs longer. Having them out of the car for longer periods of time was preferable due to the heat.

Yankee and Mollie started the session working on **call fronts** and **finish lefts**. They were working about 100 feet away from each other. At the same time, I worked with Colleen on rewarding Maggie for focusing on her upon getting out of the car (this was Colleen's first week at class with Maggie). *See Illustration 7-20a.*

Yankee was much calmer this week because there were no thunderstorms. Marie and Mark also had spent time working with Yankee during the week on **being calm in the car**. Marie had emailed me earlier in the day, suggesting that she wanted to work on just being quiet in the car for the whole session. Once they got there, though, she and Mark had decided to work on focus upon getting out of the car. He did great! It was only about two weeks ago that they got little to no focus from him; my, how quickly things can change! This all stemmed from the **parallel walking** we had done for a few weeks. The rewardable behavior in that exercise was moving forward with the handler, sniffing and occasionally checking in with the human.

Mollie had a much more difficult time of things. First of all, Kim and Don parked their car facing the opposite way they usually parked. This was enough to render Mollie incapable of functioning. She came out of the car and was initially able to work. Kim had a question about finishes, so we worked on that together for about a minute. Mollie seemed fine, but soon after that began lowering her body posture…that dangerous slippery slope toward total shutdown. Just doing finishes is something almost completely new to her; we

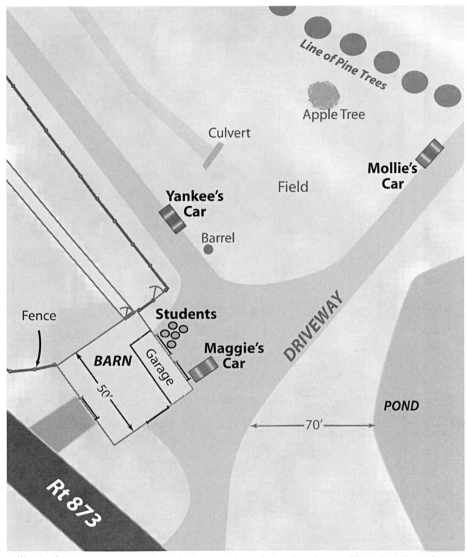

Illustration 7-20a shows the relative position of the dogs' cars. Note that there is an open garage door near the students' position where students can sit under cover or use as an entrance when classes take place inside the barn.

had worked on it briefly back in April, but it was incredibly difficult for her at that time and she never mastered it, let alone understood it. The luring toward the back of the human body was frightening and baffling to her.

While Mollie and Yankee were working, Kristen was mentoring Colleen on the specifics of getting Maggie out of the car, calling her name and clicking and treating focus. We started with her on the side of the car that faces the pond so she would be away from the people. After some fumbling, Colleen got the idea of the sequence, and then began to bring Maggie out of the near side of the car to the people. Only Kristen, Don, Laura and Mark were there, but that's plenty of people for her to ignore. Colleen was able to ask Maggie for four or five behaviors she could click and treat (curtsy seems to be her new favorite) and then **party** with her in the car. At one point Maggie went to Kristen to sniff her (oops! Colleen's leash was too long) but Kristen simply stood in a

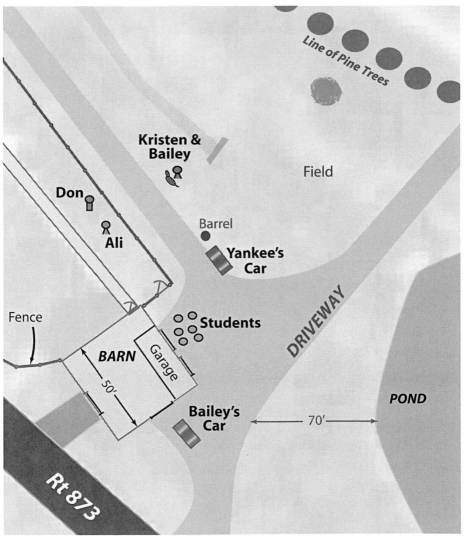

Illustration 7-20b.

neutral position and waited for Maggie to turn back to Colleen. Lots of room for improvement there, but at least Maggie didn't react to the "new" person!

Next up was Kristen and Bailey. We had discussed on the Yahoo! group what to do with Bailey's ball. He loves his ball so much that he's willing to make friends with anyone who throws it for him. This is a different version of what Tara dubbed **subsidence,** a decrease in the intensity of an emotion or behavior in the presence of a positive stimulus. So I took Bailey's ball and Don came with me. We stood on the inside of my yard fence while Kristen brought Bailey out of his car past all the humans to the other side of the driveway from where we were standing. She put him on a **longline** once she got there and took off his regular leash. She got his attention and then I called his name and threw the ball for him. He wanted to bring it back to me. (Kristen's big complaint about this is that he completely ignores her if someone else is throwing the ball...NOT what we want a reactive dog to do!) But I ignored him until he went back to Kristen and dropped the ball for a click and treat. Another issue for him is giving up the ball. She then gave it to me and I threw it again. After a few repetitions of this, I first asked him for a sit before throwing the ball. Don then had a few turns at this, with equal success. He even asked Bailey to down and he did! At one point, the ball went a bit close to Yankee's car, and Yankee barked, but Bailey didn't react a bit to the bark. Yay Bailey! They ended the game by putting the leash back on him and loose leash walking him back past all the humans in different postures, to the pond for a quick dip, then to the car. *See Illustration 7-20b.*

Now it was Spencer's turn. Laura was envious of the ball throwing and expressed interest in trying this next week. In the meantime, Linda and I stood on the inside of the fence again while Laura got Spencer out of the car. We need to start bumping Spencer's threshold again (see **subthreshold** in the Glossary). Laura's schedule had placed a huge burden on their work together and he had backslid. Laura also finds Spencer's behavior upsetting; he barks ferociously, and she is afraid he will come out of his collar or harness. So she has him on two leashes now, and she's much more relaxed about working with him. She worked him about 20 feet closer than she usually was to the group of people standing around, plus she had Linda and me nearby. Because we were behind the fence we were safe, so we could relax and so could Laura. He didn't pay the slightest bit of attention to us and worked with a waggly stump. I decided I wanted to push him a bit more since his mouth was soft. Since I was there with treats, I called his name (with Laura's permission) and when he looked at me I tossed about 15 treats directly at him. He gave me a very brief hard look and then got all excited about the treats. Laura then got his focus on her again and after a few clicks, I repeated the process. Linda then did the same thing twice. By the second time she did it, the second he heard her call his name he was clearly EXCITED to hear his name and looked happily at her, waiting for the treats!!! YAY for Spencer! Laura finished up her session by getting his focus back on her -- he was distracted by the smell of where Bailey had been standing -- so she put him back in the car without discussion, then got him back out again, got his focus and used the known "sniff area" as a reward, and then **partied in the car**.

For our second session, we had Yankee and Mollie out again with Maggie doing a repeat of the first session. By this time, Maggie was very warm in the car, so they walked her around the pond for a bit. Yankee continued to give great focus to Mark and Marie, but Mollie was shutting down. She was opting to go into her crate in the car. The warm weather was concerning me and I would have rather seen her sitting outside the car than in it, so I had Kim sit outside the car on the ground with Mollie. She spent the rest of the session lying in the grass, looking around but mostly away from everyone. Kim didn't push behaviors, and Mollie didn't offer them. I can't say I was very happy about this event, but she wasn't barking. This is a big improvement in its own way; however, given the opportunity, Kim reported that Mollie would have rather been in the car.

In retrospect, it would have been more appropriate for her to use "getting back in the car" as the reward for Mollie. Bring her out of the car, get her focus, and send her back in. Another development unfolded: since Mollie decided a few months ago that she hates the sound of the **clicker** (this after over two years of working with me!), Kim realized that perhaps what was shutting her down was the sound of the other dogs getting clicked! This is entirely possible, so next week we will work with her by herself, with only people, and make sure the radio or AC is on when she's in the car so the sound of other clickers is muffled. Kim now uses, "Yay!" as her **verbal marker** instead of the clicker.

When Yankee and Maggie were finished with their sessions, I had Bailey do another ball throwing session. This time Tracy and I were the ball throwers. Tracy is a tough-looking guy, yet Bailey had no trouble waiting patiently for the ball to be thrown. Bailey has made vast improvements in the recent past, but this was a real boon for all of us. While we were out there throwing the ball for Bailey, I suggested to Colleen that she bring Maggie out of the car (as soon as she was quiet) and sit with her close to the garage door of the barn (about ten feet behind where everyone else was sitting). This would be the next step for her in her goal of tolerating being near people. Colleen was instructed to reward focus and a "down" position. Everyone else was instructed to sit about ten feet away, chat with Tracy and Colleen, but ignore the dog. Initially, Maggie looked for someone to give her a reason to growl, but no one did, and she quickly settled into her task.

After a while we began the process of having Maggie hand target Kristen's hand. Maggie had been calm for a few minutes and, interestingly enough, she was able to touch her nose to Kristen's hand but wouldn't take the treat from her. She asked Maggie to touch again, and this time she clicked and dropped the treat on the ground. Maggie decided that the treat was okay to take from the ground. I think she was afraid to take it from a hand.

I had also suggested to Marie that she bring Yankee out of the car and sit with him at the corner of the fence line. This put him about 30 feet away from Maggie, 90 feet away from Mollie and 20 feet away from Bailey as he walked past. He was calm, laying down and making no noises with these dogs all out. Wonderful!

When Bailey was done, he loose leash walked about 20 feet away from Maggie and Yankee, who had their backs to him, without incident. Wow! He also walked between Maggie and Mollie, even though Mollie was about 90 feet away. This and walking past all those people really is a testament to his improvement.

We also repeated Spencer's session with the treat tossing. He became more enamored of the process as he went along! This time Linda and I worked with him, and he clearly looked forward to looking directly at a person and anticipating something great. What a difference from the usual loud and frightening display he normally puts on!

July Twenty-Seventh

*Present: **Kristen, Linda and Bailey; Kim, Don and Mollie; Colleen and Maggie.***
New observers: Patti, Tara and Glen (they will start with their dog, Max).
Bad weather (severe local thunderstorms) prevented others from coming.

We started our session inside with the usual pow-wow. While we were talking, Kristen brought Bailey into the training room and worked on having him lie down and pay attention to Kristen, rather than scanning the room looking for someone to bark at. He showed some minor arousal initially as he came in and looked around, but offered Kristen wonderful attention and figured out that laying down got him tons of good stuff. Initially his back was to her and he was facing the "new people," but within five minutes he was facing Kristen. Toward the end of his time, Don adjusted the position of his chair. Don was about ten feet away from Bailey. Bailey looked at Don but didn't react, and turned his attention back to Kristen. Yay!

Kim decided that she'd like to do some **calming curves** with Mollie outside, because one of Mollie's toughest situations is during a walk, when a person is approaching her. We began with a person (Colleen) standing 80 feet away from Mollie. Kim and Colleen each took three steps toward each other, and on the third step, turned away from each other. Kim's job was to click and treat Mollie the moment her attention turned away from Colleen. *See illustration 7-27a.*

At this distance, Mollie wasn't even paying attention to Colleen. Good start! We had put her in a position that allowed her to be successful. They each returned to their start point and then took four steps each before turning away. We continued this progression until Mollie and Colleen were eight feet away from each other. Mollie's body language told us clearly that she was enjoying

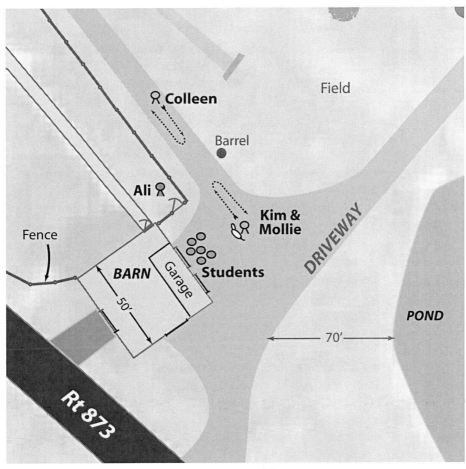

Illustration 7-27a.

this activity!

However, it occurred to me that my presence – I was standing on the other side of the fence that runs along the driveway – was having a **subsidence** effect on Mollie! After the session ended   in which Mollie appeared to be happy, with no barking at all – we discussed this as a possibility.

Maggie's turn was next. Colleen wanted to work on hand targeting, so she got Maggie out of the car and headed toward Kristen and me (we were outside). When Maggie was paying attention to Colleen, Colleen pointed to my hand and said, "Go see." At the same time, I said, "Touch," to Maggie, she targeted my hand, and I clicked and treated. I gave her several treats while she sat in front of me, and then I repeated the process backward to send Maggie to Colleen. Maggie did fine and turned back to Colleen beautifully.

Next it was Kristen's turn to do some hand targeting. Maggie did fairly well, but was distracted by the environment, and as time went on, she stopped taking food treats from us at all. Incidentally, Colleen missed two opportunities to reward Maggie for checking in with her. This could very well have made the difference in the success rate of the session; had Colleen been able to reward Maggie for checking in with her, her session might have gone better as she may have been able to maintain focus for a longer period of time.

For Bailey's second round, we brought him back into the training room and repeated what we did the first time, but with some distractions. We decided that the experience with Don moving was good practice, so we took turns being slightly distracting to Bailey. Some of us moved our arms, some stood up, some moved a chair to a different part of the room. We maintained at least a ten-foot distance from Bailey. He managed to do very well with no outbursts, but after about five minutes, the tension seemed to be accumulating and his mouth became hard. I instructed Kristen to drop his treats on the floor rather than putting them in his mouth. This forces him to lower his head and relax his jaw. She then asked him to roll over on his side. Between those two activities, Bailey's mouth became very soft and he relaxed.

Back outside, we repeated Mollie's calming curves routine, but this time with Linda. I have learned that it is good to repeat a skill twice. It allows the dog to internalize the events of that session. Mollie did very well. Again, however, I remained on the other side of the fence. We are sure that this helped Mollie to be better able to handle the situation.

Maggie also repeated her first session wherein she hand targeted both me and Kristen. Maggie was distracted by sniffing Kristen during her session, so we kept the session short and stopped before she thought too much about reacting.

August Seventeenth

Present: Marie, Mark and Yankee; Kristen, Linda and Bailey; Glen, Patti, Tara and Max; and Laura and Spencer

Today, as we have discussed in previous weeks, we have decided not to do the pow-wow portion of the class due to the increased number of people in the class. While we all love the pow-wow because it allows us to discuss pertinent topics and possible strategies, the class is currently over-full with seven dogs, and we need as much work time as possible. The Yahoo! group will take care of discussions if necessary.

We started with Yankee; Marie and Mark have realized that Yankee barks like crazy when he's in the car and a bike goes by him. They decided that they'd like to work on that a bit. With Yankee in the car, and the front and back windows covered with a sheet but the side windows open, Linda walked a bike by the car, about eight feet away from him. Marie was feeding Yankee regardless of his behavior; she was doing **classical conditioning**. The moment the bike appeared, the food and attention started happening. The moment the bike was out of sight, the food and attention stopped. Linda passed by him four times and he was fine, with soft eyes and mouth, barely looking at the bike. *See illustration 8-17a.*

Then, since the bike we were using was way too big for Linda, we had Mark ride the bike very slowly down and back. He did this eight times. Yankee was still doing great. I think some of the phenomenon of **subsidence** was taking place here; Yankee really looked at Mark on the bike rather than the bike. Mark doesn't normally ride a bike. I asked Mark to increase his speed a bit and on the second pass, Yankee barked. He barked for well over a minute, indicating that his arousal level had shot through the roof! Once Yankee was able to calm down to the point of not barking, we had Mark pass again twice, going as slowly as he did the first time. He passed four times and Yankee was

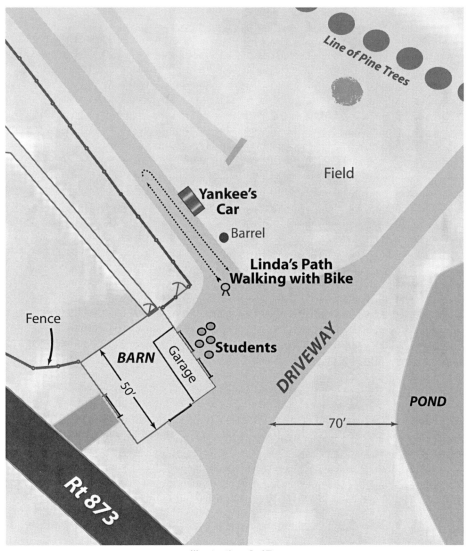

Illustration 8-17a.

fine. We ended the session. While we were unable to calculate the speed at which Mark was riding, he had a sense of how slowly he was going, and we will start there on the next session.

Kristen wanted to work on "a normal walk" in a park setting and what Bailey would see. Glen and Tara walked out to the apple tree, about 120 feet from the garage where we gather, and then Kristen began to walk Bailey. *See Illustration 8-17b.* If Bailey pulled, she stopped and waited for him to turn back and pay attention to her. If he walked nicely, she clicked and treated him. He was permitted to look around and sniff, but he had to check in with her every ten seconds or so. She was able to walk within 30 feet of them three times, and Bailey exhibited no interest in them other than wanting to visit them. Tara even swung from a branch with no repercussion! Bailey's body language remained calm, with soft eyes, and he even checked in with Kristen on several occasions (as opposed to Kristen asking for it).

Bailey then waited while Glen and Tara walked back to the garage, and

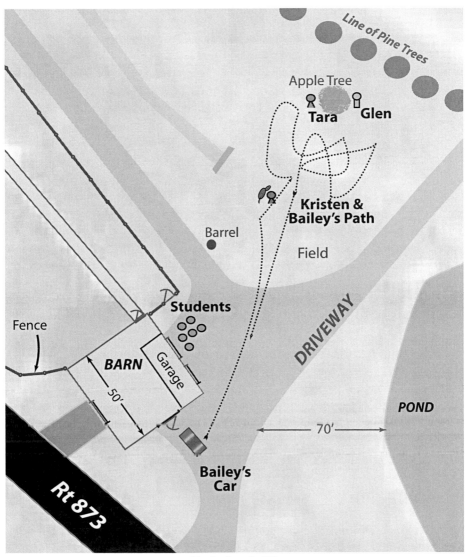

Illustration 8-17b.

then he went back to his car with lots of treats! We accomplished a lot in this session; people moving around him, near him, people in front of him, him moving toward people, and people moving toward him. The change in his behavior is really remarkable.

Then it was Max's turn. This was Max's first visit as a student to this class. Max is not accustomed to being left in the car. While he didn't make much noise, it was difficult for him. Glen began working with him by opening the car door, rewarding him for waiting, inviting him out of the car, saying his name as he landed on the ground, and waiting for him to look at Glen so he could be clicked and treated. He got Max out of the car four times to no avail. Each time, Max tried desperately to see what the folks near the barn were doing. This was a new experience for him; when he first arrived for class, he flew out of the car and ran around happily for about three minutes before we could corral him in the barn. The excitement of that episode in addition to the stress of the new environment resulted in a dog who was unable to pay attention.

On his third repetition, Max looked at Glen but had no interest in the food treat. The possibility existed that he was anxious about being separated from Patti and Tara, but they walked over to the car after the second repetition and he was still terribly distracted. After the fourth unsuccessful repetition, I set up Max's family to work on rewarding him for being calm and quiet in the car (**separation anxiety** issues). Glen started by giving him a treat through the open window, turning his back for one second, giving a treat, turning his back for three seconds, giving a treat, etc. Once he was able to turn his back for about 30 seconds, he started to take a step away and come back. Over time, the distance traveled increased until Glen is far away, out of sight. Max picked up on this very quickly.

Laura admitted that Spencer has been having a hard time in general and had been destroying some minor items such as paper when Laura was at work. She wished to just spend time rewarding him for checking in with her, regardless of what was going on around him. I suggested she walk him along the tree line (behind the apple tree, about 140 feet away from the garage). As she walked him, he checked in with her every few seconds, did lots of sits and downs for treats while wagging his stump. He was generally happy to be out and about, and took no notice of us from such a distance. At the same time, however, Glen, Tara and Patti were working on moving a distance away from Max and were visible to Spencer; they were about 80 feet away but moving around. I wanted to be sure I was able to communicate with Laura as she worked him, so I walked directly toward them as they walked. I closed in to about 60 feet and carried on a conversation with Laura. Spencer was able to look at me for a second or two and then go back to his sniffing. Wonderful! He just continued to smile and meander around, paying no attention to me at all.

For Yankee's second session, we repeated the first session, with Linda walking the bike first, for four passes. Then Mark rode the bike slowly for eight passes, and Yankee had no trouble with that. One difference in this session was that Mark rode the bike on both sides of the car because we always want to **generalize** as much as possible. Next, he rode a bit faster, and Yankee didn't bark. He appeared to be able to ignore the bike by this time. So I asked Marie to switch from classical conditioning to operant conditioning…wait for him to look at her before clicking and treating as the bike goes by. He was able to do this three times, so we stopped the session there and talked about perhaps enlisting the neighbor kid to WALK her bike on the driveway so Marie could practice.

Bailey repeated his session, too, but this time Mark and Laura were the tree-inspectors. No one swung from the tree, but Mark started juggling apples. Bailey had no problem with the intensity of this activity, even from 30 feet away. The main difference in his behavior during this session was that he pulled Kristen a lot more frequently and intensely. This was apparently a very interesting setting for him. There is no doubt that Bailey is learning that the people in the class are trustworthy and will not threaten him.

Max did much better on the second session in terms of not trying to leave the car. He was still anxious about being in the car and was still distracted by wanting to go up to the garage to see what was going on. Max needs to learn that going to visit is not his decision. But again he was very slow to look at his handler, which resulted in his returning to the car three times. Sensing that this dog might lose it from over-stimulation (not be able to pay attention to the handler at all, nor offer any behaviors), I bent the rules for him. ANY focus he put on Glen was click-worthy. We abandoned the **ten-second rule** and simply waited for Max to look at Glen. It only took three focuses before the light bulb went on and he realized that looking at dad was great. Once he looked at Glen, he got four or five treats rather than just one. Glen asked him to sit, which he did (but didn't ask him to look at him first), down, and shake. We got five clickable behaviors and then I sent the whole family there for a huge party! They need to work on focus a lot.

Spencer again did really well with his walk, coming within 60 feet of the group and acting like we weren't there. Because he was doing so well, I felt that it was time to push him. Laura is notoriously overly cautious with him because she is terrified that he will do something unacceptable. I had her come closer to the group, and he was able to come easily within 20 feet of me as I stood there talking to Laura. Excellent doggie!

August Twenty-Fourth

Present: Marie, Mark and Yankee; Colleen and Maggie; Kristen, Linda and Bailey; Tara, Patti, Glen and Max. Debbie observed.

Today we started with Yankee; we worked on moving stimuli again. With Yankee in the car and Marie standing outside the car, I jogged past the car four times while Marie fed Yankee each time he saw me, for as long as he saw me. Linda then jogged at the same pace twice, and then Kristen jogged by twice, as well. Yankee had no problems with joggers, so we moved on to the bike.

Mark walked the bike by the car six times, and Yankee's mouth was initially hard. It got a bit softer, so we moved on to the bike ride. Mark rode the bike slowly by for four passes, and then a bit faster for another four passes. Yankee didn't bark at all, and was perfectly contented to take treats from Marie. **

Colleen and Maggie were planning on working on accepting attention and hands of strangers. The plan was to get her out of the car and bring her over to me so that we could do some send-offs, and then have her do it with others. Colleen got Maggie out of the car, and her attention was tenuous, at best. Colleen asked her to target, and Maggie was unable to comply within the ten-second limit, so she returned to her car for a few minutes.

On their second attempt, as they walked closer to me (from the car to the barn, where we were all sitting), Maggie's attention diminished to the point where she was sniffing everything. I was not convinced that this was completely distraction. I got the sense that she was nervous and using sniffing as a **displacement behavior** or **calming signal**. Colleen barely managed to maintain Maggie's attention until she got to us. When Maggie looked at

---

**Several days later, Marie emailed to the group that she was speechless. Apparently some kids were yelling and screaming and riding their bikes past his house. Yankee didn't make a peep!

Colleen, she pointed to my hand, told her to "go visit"; Maggie targeted my hand, got clicked but would not take food. Colleen was instructed to verbally praise her. We continued to do this with Kristen. Maggie was only able to target Kristen's hand three out of four times but would not take food, and chose instead to check in with Colleen. While this seems to be less than perfect, I instruct my students that under every circumstance, if someone else is asking their dogs to do something but instead they check in with the owners, they are to have a party!! It is WAY more important for our reactive dogs to choose to pay attention to us than everything else in their environment. Yay, Maggie!

Kristen and Bailey spent their session walking past people in ones and twos. They walked up and down the long driveway, passing people within about an eight foot distance with Bailey paying attention to Kristen. He has little trouble with women, a bit of trouble with men, and the least trouble with small people. This held true in tonight's session. He did not lunge at anyone, but he had little trouble with Tara, who is very petite, and substantially more trouble with Mark, who is tall. What an excellent improvement over even a few months ago!

Patti worked with Max. Their car was quite a distance from where everyone was hanging out at the barn, and when Patti got Max out of the car, he was very interested in what was going on. She wisely took him to the front of the car (away from the people) and I instructed her to simply wait until he looked at her, even if it wasn't at her face. For about 2½ minutes, he increasingly was able to look at her but wasn't able to take treats. He did lots of whining. Suddenly, he was able to respond to a sit cue, then a down cue, then paw, spin, sit and down again! Wow! I suggested to Patti that she sit in the car with him for a while. Max's separation anxiety makes it difficult for him to remain in the car alone.

Yankee's second session involved Mark driving their car up and down the driveway (backward and forward) while Marie fed Yankee, who was in the back seat. We did four passes of Yankee riding in the car, passing a bike which was stationary. Because he tolerated that well, with a **soft mouth**, no hard looking and no barking, we continued to work on this for four passes with the car moving and the bike moving, as well. This elicited a bark from Yankee. But only one. Good boy!

Colleen and Maggie repeated their session with the send-offs. Maggie was able to do send-offs with me and take the food. We then had Maggie do send-offs with Kristen, and Maggie was able to complete the task without losing her focus. By the time we asked her to do send-offs with Linda, we had lost her focus. Shame on us! We asked for too long a session. We were greedy trainers!

I asked Glen to drive his car up close to the rest of us at the barn. *See Illustration 8-24a.* Max's behavior is not quite the same as the other dogs in this category in that he does not react to fear by barking and lunging. Because Max is so uncomfortable about being left in the car, by the time he gets out of the car and settles down, his allotted class time is up. So instead, I had Glen get Max out of the car, get his attention, then walk him up to be near the rest of

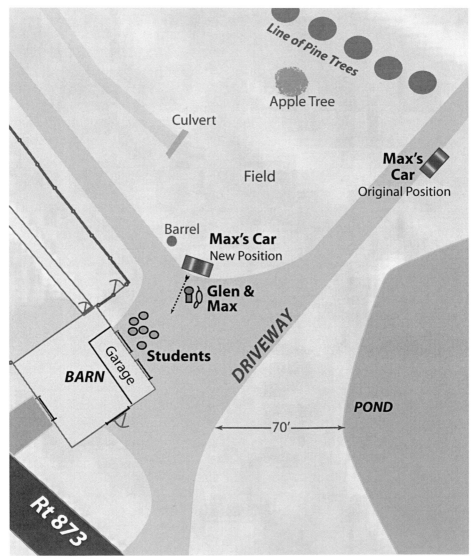

Illustration 8-24a.

the people. He was very curious and did a lot of approach/avoidance with the people, their shoes, the chairs, etc. Rather than ask him to do something and give him ten seconds to complete the task, I did not set a time limit at all. This time, we just let him sniff and approach. Each time he did this, Glen praised him. He was fairly happy to see me but also enjoyed investigating others' shoes. We ignored him for the most part, which allowed him to investigate with little expectation. Max was out there for at least five minutes. My experience tells me that this will enable him to learn about his environment so that when we do more advanced concepts with Max, he will be able to assimilate it all more effectively.

August Thirty-First

Present: Marie and Yankee; Kristen, Linda and Bailey; Kim, Don and Mollie; Debbie and Elvis; Tara, Glen, Patti and Max; Colleen and Maggie.

Tonight, Marie knew immediately what she wanted to work on: bikes and the car! With Yankee in the car, Marie stood outside the car while Kristen walked the bike at a normal walking pace back and forth past the car. She did this four times. Yankee was calm with a soft mouth. Kristen increased her pace to a brisk walk with the bike past the car for another four passes. Yankee was still calm, didn't bark, and was able to take treats nicely. I then volunteered to ride the bike past the car. At first I rode very slowly for four passes, and then increased my pace to a moderately slow pace for six passes, with the last two passes being even faster. Yankee's mouth continued to be manageable, and he did not bark at all. We decided that this was a good place to stop for this session because it signified an improvement in what he had been able to do only a week ago.

Kristen wanted to continue practicing walking Bailey past people in a park-like setting, and Debbie wanted to start out slow with Elvis for his first week at class. So they worked at the same time but at opposite ends of the property. The following is what each did:

Kristen got Bailey out of the car and loose leash walked him toward the culvert and the apple tree. She walked past me, Patti and Tara. Kristen requested Tara because she is of small stature and Bailey has shown that he is less reactive to "small people" (i.e., kids). The thinking here is that Tara serves as a source of subsidence for the fact that this was the first time we were walking by him in a group of more than two. He did great! He was smiling and happy, taking treats with a soft mouth (unusual for Bailey!) and checking in with Kristen on her own. After that pass, Kristen continued to walk around

Tara and Patti while I went to see how Debbie and Elvis were doing.

Debbie warned me that Elvis was having a tough day; indeed, he was having a difficult time paying attention to Debbie. She had to put him back in the car almost immediately because he barked at Bailey. She gave him about 20 seconds in the car and then brought him back out again. He looked at her, got clicked and treated, but then barked again, and went back into the car. When she was ready to bring him out again, he leapt out of the car before he was invited, so she had to put him back in the car again!

At this time, I asked Kristen to walk behind the barn and out of view from Elvis for a bit more of her walk. When I did this, Kristen took her attention off of Bailey to look at me, and Bailey lunged at Patti and Tara. This resulted, of course, in Bailey going back to his car.**

Debbie brought Elvis out again. This time he was much more able to focus on Debbie, but his mouth was very hard despite the fact that there were no dogs present. Remember, stress is cumulative. Debbie wanted to reinforce focus on her in the presence of people nearby (good plan!). We had three people walking nearby along the driveway. She was able to ask him to do about 15 clickable behaviors, and he responded within a few seconds each time. He seemed to want to approach Linda, who was out of Bailey's car by now, but suddenly found himself frightened of her. Linda's response was to crouch down to make herself smaller, but Elvis continued to bark and growl at her. Of course, Debbie put him back in the car. I suggested that perhaps because Linda's front was facing Elvis, he interpreted that as a continuing assault. Sometimes a feature of a person or a posture can seem insignificant to us, but intense and scary to a dog. We will have to reintroduce Elvis and Linda. Also, sometimes, I find that once a dog has decided that something is scary, it's really difficult to interrupt that behavior. Removing the dog from the situation and starting over at a less intense level will be the key. One more thing: people in these classes have learned to move slowly, sideways, and without eye contact. While this is appropriate dog body language, it occasionally seems to create suspicion in a new dog!

Kim and Mollie worked on calming curves. This is something they'd

---

**It should be noted that at the beginning of class, Bailey chewed a headrest in Kristen's car. Kristen and Bailey have been battling separation anxiety for a long time. For reasons that Kristen couldn't explain, Bailey had a setback today, so she asked her mom, Linda, to sit in the car with him. Despite this setback, he had been doing very well during his session, including completely ignoring Elvis' barking, until Kristen took her attention off of her task at hand.

done quite a while ago, and Kim remembered that Mollie enjoyed it. We had Colleen start about 50 feet away from Kim and Mollie. They walked three steps toward each other, then turned away. Kim clicked Mollie when she turned her head away from Colleen. This wasn't difficult to do, as Mollie was happily looking around at everyone who was present! They each walked back to their starting points, and then walked four steps toward each other. Mollie appeared to be happy and sniffing around, even as the distance between her and Colleen diminished. Certainly, she was checking out her visual environment as she sniffed, but did not give off any visual signs of stress in the process. They went five steps, six steps, seven steps, eight steps, then eight steps with Mollie on a shorter leash. Now she was starting to pay attention to Colleen! Even at nine steps, she was doing just fine. At ten steps, and on a short leash (because the gap between them was only about three feet), Mollie checked in twice with Kim. At 11 steps, Mollie did a double take toward Colleen, then checked in with Kim! Yay, Mollie! She figured out the game…see the person approaching you and check in with Mom! The distance between Mollie and Colleen was less than three feet! And no barking!

This week, Glen parked his car a bit closer to the barn. When he got Max out of the car, he was initially unable to take food from Glen, so I instructed him to click and praise more than anything else. He offered Max a treat after every few clicks to use as a barometer for his emotional status. We had decided two weeks ago to remove the ten-second criteria for Max, since being in the car was an anxiety producing behavior, and a behavior on which they are working at home and at class. When Max is in the car, one of the three family members is always rewarding him for being calm and quiet in the car. By the time he gets out of the car for his turn, he is fairly aroused. Giving him whatever time he needs to calm down enough to check in with the person at the other end of the leash appears to be critical for him. The difference between Max and the other dogs in the class is that he is more fearful than he is reactive. I quickly realized that his criteria are, therefore, different.

After about 2½ minutes of standing outside the car, Max was starting to (ever so briefly) check in with Glen. His focus was on the group of people hanging out near the barn. The reasonable thing to do, since he's afraid of people, was to use the **Premack principle**! Here we have two behaviors, one more likely to occur (move toward the people) and one less likely to occur (look at Glen). So each time he looked at Glen, Glen clicked and took one step toward the people. This makes sense since he wasn't taking food. While I didn't time it, the latency of focus diminished over the course of the "walk" until he got within about 15 feet of them. At this point, fear began to overtake curiosity. The other students were instructed to have a normal conversation (not difficult for them!) and completely ignore Max. Over a period of five minutes, he worked his way up to the people using a very conflicted approach-avoidance pattern and began to sniff their feet, hands and chairs. Each time he looked at Glen, Glen clicked and offered him a treat, which he refused with only two exceptions. He was able to take a few treats from me, and then when he looked at Glen, I instructed him to click and run away toward his car, and allow him to walk near the pond and sniff around for a few minutes before going back into the car for a party.

Colleen and Maggie came this week with wonderful treats and were ready to do better than last week! Colleen was instructed to get Maggie's focus through a few clicks and treats, and then I instructed her on how to do **send-offs**. Both Colleen and Maggie initially had a hard time with the mechanics of this exercise but improved with a few repetitions. The idea here is that since Maggie is afraid/suspicious of hands, teaching her to target the hands of people will **counter condition** the fearful response. When Maggie looked at Colleen, Colleen took a step in my direction, pointed to my outstretched hand, and said, "Go see." She waited for Maggie to target my hand with her nose when I said, "Touch!", clicked, and then called Maggie back to give her a treat. Initially, Maggie wanted to sniff my hand, my legs, etc. With repetition and more proactive direction from Colleen, Maggie began to understand her task. In effect, we asked Maggie to do something very difficult by targeting, but she has recently learned that targeting is fun, AND we took the pressure off her by then having Colleen call her away from the hand. It's really important for the dog to understand exactly what's expected of her so she can be successful. If it's not really clear, the dog becomes stressed; this often results in a reactive outburst. Not a good idea!

Maggie hand targeted me three times and went back to Colleen for a treat, and then did the same for Kristen. She appeared to be calm, so we increased the challenge for her. Colleen indicated that she'd be thrilled if Maggie would take a treat from Kristen this week, so we had Maggie hand target me and I clicked and treated her, sending her back to Colleen after each target. Then we did exactly this same thing with Maggie and Kristen. Maggie had no trouble at all taking food from Kristen! It is important to realize that taking food from Colleen is easier for Maggie than taking food from a stranger.

For Yankee's second round, Linda jogged past Yankee in his car for four repetitions, then Kim jogged by the car for six repetitions, and finally Colleen jogged past the car for six repetitions. Each time, Yankee was able to take treats with a soft mouth and didn't bark at all. It was a fairly short session but an important one; this would almost certainly have resulted in a barking fit only a few weeks ago.

In addition to this work, Marie had Yankee out of the car for a few of the other dogs' sessions. She kept him just inside the garage of the barn, while each other dog worked outside at varying distances. Yankee remained calm throughout the sessions.

Kristen and Bailey chose to spend some time walking between Linda and me down the driveway. We walked past a group of four people and he was calm, checking in with Kristen, taking treats with a soft mouth, keeping a loose leash. We chose Linda and me because we are the most familiar people to him other than Kristen. As such, we could have had a subsidence effect on the group of four people. He had never walked past a group of four people in the class before, nor had he ever walked sandwiched in between two other people. We had just made two variables more difficult at the same time (greedy of us) and he was able to tolerate it quite well.

Meanwhile, Debbie and Elvis worked again while the group of four people walked about at varying distances from him. They approached him and walked away, and walked perpendicular to him. The closest the people came was 15 feet. Bailey was visible to him from a distance of about 80 feet again, but the duration of visibility was shorter. Elvis was able to tolerate this session much more calmly than the last one and without barking. Excellent!

Kim and Mollie did some more calming curves, but this time with two people (Tara and Patti). Again, we started at a distance of about 50 feet, and they each walked toward each other for three steps, then turned away and returned to their starting points. Mollie has never done this with two people before, and we suspected that it would be difficult for her. She had no problems with 3, 4, 5, 6, 7, or 8 steps. But her focus wasn't on Kim. Actually, nor was it on Tara and Patti. So, we repeated eight steps, but this time Kim made sure to wait for Mollie to look at her before clicking and treating her, and continued this process for the rest of the session.

At ten steps, Mollie's mouth was a bit harder and she did a double check of the two women. At 11 steps, she did a double take toward both the women and Kim, so we repeated 11 steps and it was easier for her. Because of the proximity of Mollie to the women at this point (only about four feet), we did a "walk by," meaning they simply walked past each other. Mollie was able to do this with no trouble, so we repeated it for the sake of reinforcing the behavior.

Feeling a bit greedy and like we needed to push Mollie a bit more, we went back to only walking ten steps toward each other, but at the apex of their turn, Tara and Patti both said, "Hi" to Kim before they turned around. Mollie barked just once, and then turned away. A repeat of this step resulted in a repeat of the bark. They then regressed to taking only nine steps and saying, "Hi," and

Mollie still barked. Don remarked that it was almost as if Mollie was "saying 'hi' in return." We repeated this process again, but this time only taking eight steps. Mollie did not bark. Feeling like we'd worked her enough, we stopped there and Kim had a party for Mollie.

Patti and Max repeated the same thing Glen and Max did in the first session. The amount of time it took Max to figure out to check in with Patti had diminished by about 30 seconds! Each time he checked in with Patti, she clicked and took one step closer to the group of people he wanted to see. He was clearly calmer and more focused, panting less, and offering more focus. He quickly got to the group, and each time he looked at a person, that person said his name and tossed a treat at him. Max was able to take food that was tossed from me, Kristen, Don, and Colleen. What a huge improvement over the first session! Patti had a hard time getting Max away from us!

It is important to note that there are two major variables in play here. The first is the handler; Max is more frightened of Glen (and men in general) than he is of Patti. The second is familiarity; once a dog has done something, the second opportunity is easier. Because of these variables, we should not be surprised that Max did better the second time around. Still, it was exciting to see.

Colleen and Maggie did more send-offs. First, Maggie targeted my hand, Colleen clicked and Maggie turned back to Colleen for a treat. We did this three times and then had Kristen do the same. Just like the first session, we then had Maggie touch my hand and I clicked and treated her. We did this three times, and then Kristen did the same.

Because she was doing so well with this we brought in Kim, with whom Maggie has never interacted. We had Colleen ask Maggie to target Kim's open palm, get clicked, then turn back to Colleen. We did this three times. Then Maggie was able to target Kim's hand and get clicked and treated from Kim's hand. All of these interactions occurred within ten feet of the group! This represents a very quick improvement in Maggie's behavior in a short period of time.

September Seventh

Present: Kim, Don, DJ and Mollie; Marie, Mark and Yankee; Kristen, Linda and Bailey; Tara, Patti and Max.

Tonight, Marie stated that she wanted to continue to work with Yankee and his issues in the car. They are going on vacation with both of their dogs, and she reported that our recent work with Yankee in the car is helping him to stay calm and quiet. Their biggest issue involves anyone moving when he is in the car; this includes joggers, dogs, bikes, etc.

So tonight we had Mark and Marie sit in their car with Yankee in the back seat, and we all walked around the car, tossing treats. *See Photo 9-07a.* Initially, we all moved around at the same time, but it was entirely too stimulating for him. This was my error; Yankee is very people-friendly and I

Photo 9-07a. We took turns walking past Yankee in the car, tossing treats in the open window.

failed to recognize that this level of stimulation would, indeed, create a barking response. So we backed off and had one person at a time walk by the car and toss treats into the open window, then come by the other side of the car and do the same. Yankee seemed to have a bit more of a difficult time with the men in the group than the women.

Kim wanted to continue with Mollie and her **calming curves**. She feels that Mollie seems to like this exercise, and it helps her to deal with the people who approach them on a walk. Tonight, we had Mark do the calming curves with Mollie. She has always had a tougher time with men, and a hard time with Mark in the past (barking at him).

We started the session with them about 75 feet away from each other. *See Photos 9-07b through 9-07d.* They each took four steps toward each other, then turned away and returned to their original starting points. Mollie had no trouble with this at all, and happily checked in with Kim each time Kim turned and called Mollie. We repeated this with 5, 6, 7 steps. At eight steps, she was focused on me and doing her silly body wag, but was able to respond to Kim when she called her and paid no attention to Mark at all.

Then we did nine steps and then ten. At ten, she looked at Mark; at 11, she looked twice at him, but still was able to work. By 14 steps, amazingly, she looked hopefully toward Mark as if he had treats for her! At 15 steps, Marie got Yankee out of the car, which was behind Mark, and Mollie ignored him, but looked

Photo 9-07b. Kim and Mollie start about 75 feet away from Mark, taking an increasing number of steps toward each other. Mollie is distracted by me, but is ignoring Mark.

Photo 9-07c. Mark approaches Mollie and says "hi" as he tosses treats at her. She's looking for the treats rather than barking at him!

Photo 9-07d. Mollie has no trouble turning away from Mark and paying attention to Kim.

again at Mark in a hopeful manner! We repeated 15 steps, and had Mark say, "Hi" to Mollie as he approached. Mark had been given the instruction to toss treats at her as he approached and said hello, which he did. We decided to do this because she seemed so hopeful on previous approaches. Because of her barking, we decided to set her up for more success.

We returned to ten steps, and had Mark talk to Kim and Mollie the whole time they were approaching. The approach of a stranger no longer seemed to be the trigger for her, but the talking does. Progress! As they approached each other, Mollie "boof"ed, then turned and looked at Kim. We repeated the ten steps, and this time Mollie looked for the food Mark was tossing! At 11 steps, the result was the same, but she "boof"ed at 12 steps. When we repeated 12 steps, Mollie looked absolutely happy to see Mark! We repeated 12 steps again, and Mollie continued to look happily at Mark! Kim was really pleased with this new response, so we called it quits and Mollie had a party in her car.**

Kristen wanted to work on parallel walking with another dog, so I brought out Acacia, my Belgian Sheepdog. We walked the length of the field, which is about 200 feet long, about 100 feet apart to start with. *See Photo 9-07e.* We walked up and back four times, for a total of eight passes. With each pass, we each decreased the distance by about five feet or so. Bailey did really well with this activity; it was a new one for him. However, one end of the field is narrower than the other, and on passes six and eight, Bailey lunged toward Acacia. He was mostly quiet; he made some huffing noises but didn't bark He was able to redirect his attention to Kristen within five seconds each time. This was really a great exercise for him; Acacia paid him very little attention, so there was little for him to do but pay attention to Kristen and get clicks and treats for checking in. He has been learning to check in a lot lately!

I suggested to Patti and Tara that they continue to do with Max what they had been doing last week, and they agreed. Patti got Max out of the car and each time Max checked in with her, she clicked and took a step toward the group of people. Tonight, Max's energy was different. Rather than just pulling and staring with interest, he was actually yipping with excitement as he worked his way toward us! For a dog who finds people to be scary, this is really great!

** Tonight, Don parked right in front of the garage of the barn where we typically hang out as a group. Mollie is crated and covered in an SUV and is quiet most of the time. Don noticed that on days when they park a distance away, Mollie seems to shut down much more often. Perhaps she doesn't like to be isolated. Tonight she did great on her first session.

Photo 9-07e. Bailey and Acacia are doing parallel walking. They start at about 100 feet apart, and with each length of the field, they come about five feet closer. The goal is to have the dogs walking near each other but facing the same direction, so they are not confronting each other.

He seemed to take a bit longer to focus on Patti each time than he did during his second session last week, but once he got to the group, he was interested in sniffing around. No one was paying attention to him, so there was no pressure for him to interact. He wouldn't take food from Tara, who was in among the group. This was to be the barometer for when we could start saying his name and tossing treats at him. Max's ability to take food from a familiar person indicated that his arousal level had come down to the point where he was able to learn. We did try to toss a few treats anyway (greedy trainers!) and he did not take food. He did, however, choose to get much closer to the group than last week, and at one point, wandered into the garage, thereby cutting off his escape route. Pretty brave, we say!

Max got to a point where he started to look at Patti and then turn around as if he wanted to get away. This occurred about six minutes into the session. I instructed Patti that the next time he looked at her, she was to click him for that and run toward the car (Premack principle), but let him sniff nearby the car for a bit before putting him back into it. He is still having issues with being left alone in the car, but they take turns feeding calm and quiet behavior in the car, and also take turns sitting with him in the car. Progress in this area is slow.

Back to Marie and Yankee for their second session. We did a rerun of the first session for Yankee. We had Don, Kim, DJ, Tara, Kristen, Linda and I walking by the car and tossing treats. Slowly we started to increase our speed of movement. There was also less time in between each person. Yankee did seem to bark more at the men, but he also barked at Tara the second time she walked past. Marie and Mark were happy with the work they did with Yankee and finished their session hopeful that they would be able to use this tactic on their trip. We shall find out in two weeks!

DJ and Mollie did the second session of calming curves. Because Mollie's handler was different, we had the distraction person be the same, changing only one variable at a time. Again we started with four steps. Mollie was distracted by all of the food on the ground. We found this to be the case for steps five through eight. I then instructed DJ to move to his left (closer to the group) so she would be less distracted by things on the ground. In general, Mollie does not work as well for DJ as she does for Kim. This has been a point of frustration for all involved.

We continued with the steps and had Mark talking while walking toward them. On step nine, Mollie had no trouble with this at all. On step ten, she barked at Mark, so we went back to nine steps and she was fine. I asked them to do ten steps again, but have DJ call Mollie at step six. She turned toward him while Mark continued to move toward her, and she was able to handle this. By doing this, we helped her to disengage from the distraction before she crossed her threshold of tolerance. The next time, Mark walked ten steps but DJ called Mollie at step eight, and she was still able to handle this. He repeated this again and called her on step nine, again with great results. Then I had them both walk nine steps, and Mollie was now paying much better attention to DJ! We repeated this twice more to continue to reward it and then called it a night for Mollie.

Because it was now dark, Kristen and I were not able to do the same activity we had done the first time, so we moved within the range of the outside light and did some calming curves with Bailey and Acacia. We started about 100 feet away from each other and took five steps toward each other, then turned away. My ability to see them was diminished, but I heard lots of clicking as we worked. Kristen reported that most of the time he was checking in with her on his own, and she infrequently needed to call him. We decreased our distance, going 6, 8, 9, 10, 12, 13, 14, 16, 17, 18, and then 19 steps toward each other. We then repeated 19 steps toward each other until Bailey didn't stop to stare at us before turning away from us and moving toward Kristen; we had to repeat it six times. At 20 steps, he looked at us for a bit, then turned away and went with Kristen. Yay, Bailey! At our closest, we were 40 feet away from each other.

Tara worked with Max for his second session. We repeated exactly what we did for the first session. Max's ability to check in with Tara was much improved over his first session, and I am not sure whether it was a different handler or the lovely effect of doing the same thing twice that made the difference. The amount of time it took him to reach us was diminished, and he brought himself to within three feet of all of us. He did take tossed food from everyone who offered it and generally appeared to be much more relaxed. We ended the session the same way, with him checking in with Tara and running away from us, back to the car.

It is important to bear in mind that this dog's reaction to fear is different to most of the reactive dogs I see in the class. Max doesn't bark or lunge, he tries to hide. So we are spending our time rewarding efforts to investigate and allowing him time in this structured environment to explore on his own, while remaining within the confines of certain rules, such as checking in with his handler, no barking, etc.

September Fourteenth

Present: Kim, Don and Mollie; Kristen, Linda and Bailey; Colleen and Maggie; Tara, Patti and Max.

Because of the rain, we worked inside tonight. All of the dogs were still in their cars, but we brought them into the training room one by one.

Kim and Mollie started by doing three send-offs with Kristen. Kim had Mollie sit next to her, and when Mollie paid attention to Kim consistently (four or five times without Mollie trying to get up and go elsewhere), she took a step forward, pointed to Kristen's outstretched finger and said, "Go visit." Kristen said, "Here" at the same time and rewarded Mollie for targeting her finger. Mollie then sat (after a cue at first) and received lovely treats for sitting in front of Kristen. They then reversed the process by having Kristen point to Kim and say, "Go see Mommy," and Kim then said, "Here," and rewarded Mollie's finger target.

Mollie managed this very well, and we all remarked on how she has improved so nicely over time. We decided to have Kim do the reverse with Mollie, where Mollie sits still and allows a person to approach her and give her treats. This is a much more threatening sequence for a dog. With Mollie sitting next to Kim, Kristen started about ten feet away from Mollie. Each time Mollie looked at Kim, she used her verbal marker and treated, and Kristen took a step closer. Kim and I both watched Mollie very closely to look for visible signs that Mollie was reaching her threshold. At about the halfway mark, we both said, "Go away," to Kristen. The purpose of this was to help Mollie to understand that Kim will take care of her and to provide Mollie the opportunity to regroup before continuing this difficult work. Once Kristen was close enough, she handfed Mollie a bunch of treats. They did this three times, and while Mollie did a few double-takes, she managed to remain seated and stay quiet, as well as take treats from Kristen.

We repeated the entire process with Tara and Mollie, and Mollie's behavior was almost identical with Tara as it was with Kristen. I found this to be remarkable because Mollie has known Kristen for about 1½ years and has known Tara for only a few weeks. Since Mollie is a typical undersocialized dog, one would expect her acceptance of Tara to take much longer than it has. This is exciting!

Kristen and Bailey worked on a similar set of expectations. Going up to other class members has not been an option until now, so this was all new for him. It's only been in the past few months that we've been doing much in the way of walking around Bailey. Prior to that, he was way too reactive to be able to come closer than about ten feet.

When Kristen came into the room, I instructed her to just stand at the entrance and click and treat any attempts at focus on her. *See Illustration 9-14a.* She worked on voluntary eye contact for approximately three minutes before she stepped closer into the room. We then started with three send-offs with me. He and I have been doing this for quite some time, and his sticking point was

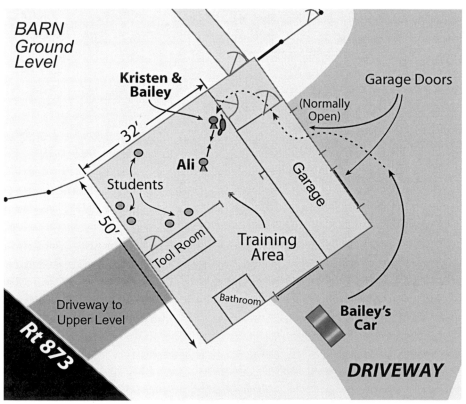

Illustration 9-14a.

always that he'd sniff my pants or legs, then look up and bark a menacing bark at me. I could also never point back to Kristen because that hand over his head was a trigger point for him. Turning one's back on him resulted in a lunge/bark from him as well. But this time, we did three send-offs, and he did great each time. He sniffed my legs the second time but his eyes were soft, as they have been for months, and he was quite happy to be doing this.

They did this with Kim as well. Kristen had to call Bailey back to her after his first two visits with Kim to avoid the hand over his head, but the third time Kim pointed a bit at Kristen and Bailey did not react. Kim was not completely comfortable with putting her hand over his head, and understandably so. Bailey's bark is fierce, and we want him to be successful in this endeavor!

Colleen was the third person to work with Bailey on this routine. He sniffed her the first time, but did not look up and bark at her. His eyes remained soft and he seemed to be enjoying the activity. They did the send-off three times, and we decided that this was a great session for Bailey and we should stop there.

Maggie's turn. *See Photos 9-14b and 9-14c.* Colleen brought her into the room, worked her on focus a bit (Maggie loves to curtsey for rewards!) and then we did the same send-offs that everyone else had been doing. I started by doing three with her. Since Maggie and I have done the private lessons

Photos 9-14b and 9-14c. Maggie is distracted, so Colleen gives the cue, '"Here." Maggie targets Colleen's finger, gets clicked and treated, then sits for a click and treat. Great focus!

together, she had little trouble with me. She followed finger targets and ate treats from me without hesitation.

Kristen then did three send-offs, and she was doing well. *See Photos 9-14d and 9-14e.* But Tara walked into the room (she had been checking on Max) and Maggie growled at her. This gave Colleen an opportunity to call her back

Photos 9-14d and 9-14e. Maggie is doing fine when Kristen uses a finger target and then treats her, but when she asks for a hand target, Maggie shows signs of stress with her whale eye.

and reward her for paying attention to Colleen. This process took about three minutes. Maggie apparently has trouble with kids (Tara is an adult of small stature), so this provided an unexpected chance to work on this behavior. After this episode, Colleen and Kristen returned to send-offs, and Maggie was able to do this with no further problems.

Tara was slated to work with Colleen, but she was a bit leery of working with Maggie, and rightly so. If Maggie sensed that Tara was unsure of her, it would have caused problems, so Don stepped in. Maggie did three send-offs with Don with no problems at all. Good for Maggie! This represents a new big step for Maggie!

Patti brought Max into the room. It took him less than two minutes to start taking treats from her and then from Tara. *See Photos 9-14f and 9-14g.* Once he established some eye contact, Patti let him just wander around the room. If he made eye contact with a person, they said his name, then clicked and tossed a treat at him. We did this for about five minutes. I then offered him a treat from my hand. He took it and a few more, and then when he looked at Kristen, she offered him a treat from her hand and he took it.

He still reaches out as far as he can with the weight on his back legs and tail tucked much of the time, but he is becoming more and more interested in who these people are. By allowing him to look around and receive good

 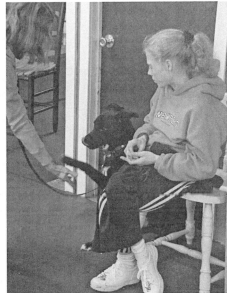

Photos 9-14f and 9-14g. The amount of time Max needs to initially pay attention to Patti is decreasing. Once he looks at Patti, he goes to Tara for treats. Note Max's whale eye and stress lick while giving his paw.

things from strangers, we are encouraging him to reach out rather than recoil. Once he is taking food happily from everyone, we will start to add some more expectations to the program.

For Mollie's second session, she did three perfect send-offs with Kristen. She then did three more greetings where she stayed seated next to Kim and Kristen approached her. Again, she was worried but was able to hold it together. She began the process of doing the same with Colleen, but on the first try, Kim accidentally stepped on Mollie's toe. Mollie squealed and shut down, so her session ended. Mollie has become quite good at telling Kim when she's had enough and is finished working, and Kim has become very good at reading Mollie. What an excellent team!

Bailey continued to astonish us with his newfound tolerance. Kim did three more send-offs with him, and Colleen followed suit. Nothing of issue to report here; Bailey did exactly what he was supposed to do. I then did the approaching greeting and he was fine with it, but then Kim did the approaching greeting and he was STILL fine! Bailey is learning the game!!

With Maggie, we did send-offs again, but this time we used a hand target instead of a finger target. Maggie's challenge is to accept strangers' hands, so this is the next step in the process. She did three send-offs with me and then

Photo 9-14h. I did some classical conditioning with Maggie to help her associate hands with good things.

three with Don. She didn't show any **whale eye** at all and took treats nicely.

I then began the classical conditioning process of holding my hand near her head and treating her. *See Photo 9-14h.* I began to explain it to everyone when a man walked into the room. Maggie began to growl/bark at him. I instructed Colleen to wait for Maggie to look at her. She could only say Maggie's name if Maggie wasn't barking; otherwise, she wouldn't have heard. It took Maggie about three minutes to be able to turn around and pay attention to Colleen instead of the man.

When this episode ended, I resumed a bit of my hand work, finished my explanation of it and ended the session. By that time, Maggie had done a lot of work and took a few treats pretty hard, and her eyes weren't as calm as they had been prior to the barking.

For Max's second session, Tara repeated the first session. Max suddenly had a much higher level of ability to turn away from the distraction and pay attention to Tara. He focused in on Tara in less than a minute. Rather than have him look around and get treats, we waited for him to look at one person. That person would repeatedly reward him for looking at him or her. He did this with Colleen, then me, then Kim and Don (who were sitting very close together), and ended up lying in a down position, receiving treats from all who adored him! Lying down is exciting because a very stressed dog can't lie down. YAY, Max! *See Photos 9-14i and 9-14j on the next page.*

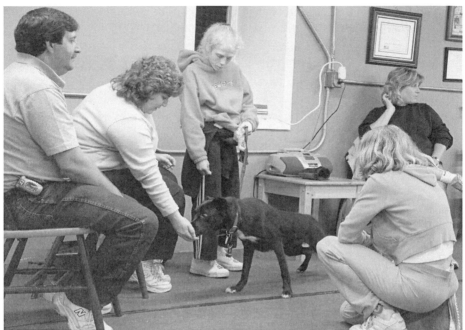

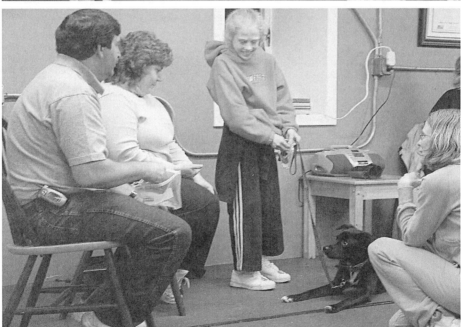

Photos 9-14i and 9-14j. Max stretches out as far as he can to get the treat from Kim while staying a safe distance away. Within a minute, he is offering to lay down for treats.

September Twenty-First

Present: Kim, Don and Mollie; Marie and Yankee; Kristen, Linda and Bailey; Tara, Patti and Max.

Marie began tonight's class by sharing her experiences of their vacation; Yankee did very well in the car on the trip. Since we are fighting the sunset, Kim wanted to start work right away on some calming curves with Mollie and people. There was some discussion as to who should be the people to walk toward her. I seem to be such a distraction for Mollie, but we can use my presence to subside the impact of a less familiar person. We agreed to have Marie and me be the walking and talking people. Mollie has become quite capable of walking toward a person if the person is quiet. As soon as the person speaks, she begins to bark. For Mollie, having two people approaching and talking to each other and to Kim is a real challenge. Having me be one of the people makes it easier for her from the anxiety perspective, but perhaps not the focus perspective!

We began at the usual distance, around 80 feet away, and took three steps toward each other. From this distance, people are usually a non-issue for Mollie, but it's always good to begin easy. We steadily diminished our distance from each other by increasing the number of steps we took toward each other, up to 14 steps. At this proximity, I was able to say hello and pet Mollie. Marie asked Mollie to sit, and Mollie sat and took a treat from Marie. Marie began to talk to Mollie, and Mollie barked. Oops! We hadn't really broken our plan down into small enough steps, and did too many things at a time. When we are sitting down, Mollie can go up to anyone in the class, sit and take treats, but this scenario is much more difficult because the humans are standing.

We repeated the 14 steps, but this time Kim did a send-off to me, called her back, then did a send-off to Marie. Mollie was fine for Marie for her send-off, targeted Marie's finger, sat and took a treat, but upon receiving the second treat, Mollie barked. This reminded us to have very short expectations of Mollie in a new situation. We ended her session there because we had been working for a while. Although Mollie barked, she was still able to return to Kim and pay attention.

Kristen and Marie liked my suggestion of having one dog inside the training room and have a second dog come into the room. Initially, I was imagining Yankee being able to handle coming into the room with Acacia sitting or laying down, paying attention to me. But Kristen liked that idea for a goal for Bailey, too, so we decided to try having them work off each other. Turns out it wasn't such a great idea.

We began with having Bailey in the back of the room, laying down and paying attention to Kristen. Right away, it was clear that this criterion was difficult for Bailey; he wanted to sit instead of lying down. When he did lay down, he laid sideways to Kristen so he could see her and the door. This was our first mistake: not having Bailey set up for success. Marie came in with Yankee. *See Photos 6-21a through 9-21c.* Her instructions were to have Yankee sit outside the training room and focus on Marie. When Marie opened the door, he was to wait for her cue to go in, and the moment he crossed the threshold she was to call his name so he'd turn back and look at her within a few seconds. Of course, the moment a dog crosses the threshold, he or she can see the contents of the room. The challenge is to do so much work with your dog that the dog learns to trust the owner. Yankee did this just fine; he whined a bit but turned and looked at Marie within about three seconds. She clicked and treated him, then began to ask him to do other things.

It was at this point that Bailey wasn't able to focus on Kristen anymore. *See Photos 9-21d through 9-21g.* He did some spectacular lunging and huffing, but little barking and growling. He was so aroused that there was no getting his "thinking brain" back. Marie took Yankee out of the room, gave him a break for about a minute or so, then brought him back in once Bailey had settled down again. Marie repeated the door etiquette routine, and Yankee was managing himself nicely, but it was again too much for Bailey, who started barking again.

We had Marie and Yankee leave, and they switched places with Kristen and Bailey. Yankee came into the room and started begging treats off of Don! He and Marie sat at the back of the room while Kristen worked on door etiquette with Bailey. Once he came into the room, Kristen got his attention, and began to ask him for things that she could click and treat. She clicked six behaviors, took him out the door, and then came back in again. He did fine for about five seconds, and then Yankee barked at Bailey. Bailey barked back for about five seconds, and then Kristen took him outside.

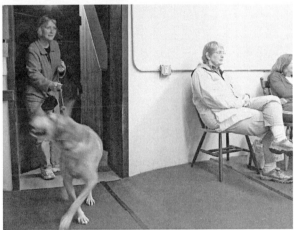

Photos 9-21a through 9-21c. Marie tells Yankee it's okay to go into the room. The second he crosses the threshold of the door, she calls him. He immediately turns toward her and sits in front of her, giving her complete focus. Notice Yankee's high head in the top photo.

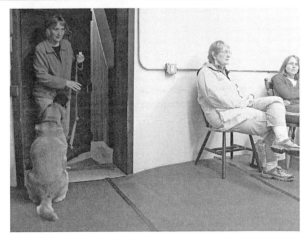

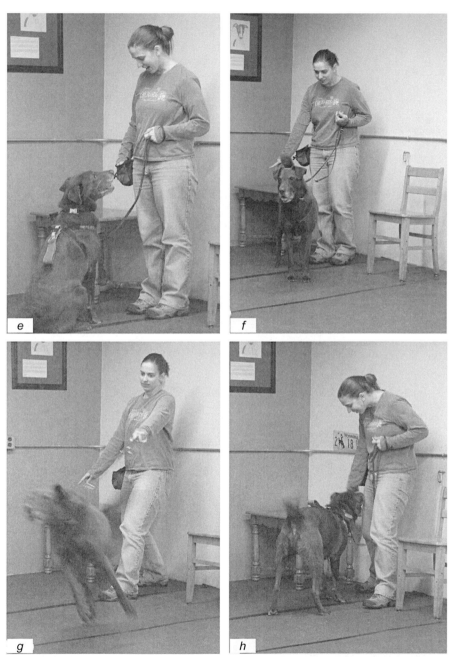

Photos 9-21e through 9-21h. (e) Kristen brings Bailey into the room, has him face her and away from the door, and rewards focus. (f) The moment Yankee enters the room, Bailey goes on alert, then goes super threshold. (g) He does little barking but lots of lunging. (h) Kristen is able to call him back to her.

Yankee barked continuously for about two minutes after Bailey left; big, loud, repetitive barks. Marie eventually backed her way into a nearby closet, where he was finally able to pay attention to her. This training session had Yankee unraveled. Marie reported that this behavior is typical for Yankee when he is in his reactive mode; most of the students in the class tease Marie, saying he's not reactive, because they have never seen Yankee bark at another dog until now! I realized almost immediately that we didn't follow through with my original intent for the exercise, which was to bring the dog into the room, get his attention, click and treat, and leave, then repeat this several more times. Short, quick repetitions of the same behavior definitely help the dog to become comfortable with the environment and expectations, and reinforce what he should be doing. Darn. Trainer and instructor error! Ah well, it happens. We'll make it right in the next session.

Patti brought Max into the training room, waited for him to look at her and clicked each time. Max had no interest in the food treat the first five clicks. The sixth time he looked at Patti, she sent him to see Tara. This was prearranged, knowing he wouldn't want food initially, knowing that he would be happy to see Tara and probably take food from her. He went to Tara and sat next to her, looking quite worried. He did, however, take food from Tara, and then from Patti. This is our indication that he's likely to take food from the others in the room. The next person he looked at would say his name, then toss him a treat. The intermediate goal is to take treats from peoples' hands; the long term goal is to tolerate touching. Max looked at Kristen, so she said his name and tossed him treats. The treats ended up falling within one foot of Kristen's feet, and Max was able to take them!

Next, Max looked at Don, who said Max's name and tossed him treats. *See Photos 9-21h through 9-21j.* Max was leery of Don but was able to interact with him so long as Max was within the safety zone of Tara. Max did manage to take treats that fell within two feet of Don, but his weight was on his back legs as he really stretched to reach the treats in a very tentative fashion. We decided that this would be a nice way to end the session for Max. He had really reached out and done something scary for him, and we wanted to end with a success, of course.

Normally, I like to do two of the same sessions for each dog per class, but because it was now dark, we brought Mollie back inside and worked on send-offs, like we did last week. We began with three send-offs to me. Kim started with Mollie sitting next to her. When she looked at Kim, Kim pointed toward me and told her to "go see." I held out my finger for Mollie to target, marked and rewarded, asked her to sit, marked and rewarded, then sent her back to Kim in the same way. We then did three repetitions of me walking up to Mollie

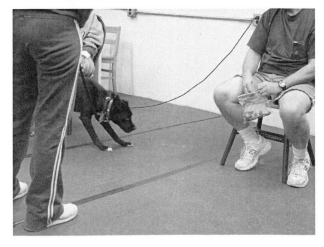

Photos 9-21h through 9-21j. Max prefers to be near Tara for comfort. When he looks at Don, Don says Max's name and tosses him a treat. Max does a combo of a play bow and a fear stance (weight on back legs), showing that he is conflicted. Eventually he becomes brave enough to stretch for a treat which has fallen about two feet away from Don.

to say hello and pet her. I started about ten feet away from her; Mollie was sitting next to Kim, facing me. Each time Mollie looked at Kim, Kim marked and rewarded. Each time I heard the mark ("Yay"), I took a step closer. When I got to arm length distance, I asked to give the dog a treat.

Kim then repeated this entire process (three send-offs and three walk-ups) with Linda. Mollie was fine with the send-offs; she's becoming a pro at this! But for the walk-ups, Mollie was a bit subdued the first two times. Her eyes were a bit wide and she looked at Linda and back to Kim with more hesitation than when she had done it with me. But the third time, she was excellent! No hesitation at all! The big difference between last week's version of this and this week's is that this week, the person walking up to Mollie didn't turn and walk away to take the pressure off at a distance of about five feet! Yay for Mollie!

Mollie did the same routine a third time, this time for Marie. Mollie showed a bit of whale eye for Marie, but was still able to take treats from her. We did the walk-ups again, but only did two, as the session was rather long with lots of repetition for Mollie. She was doing well, and we wanted to end on a good note for her.

We repeated the session with Bailey and Yankee again, but first we discussed what went wrong with the first session and made a more distinct plan. We started with Yankee in the corner of the room, focusing on Marie. Kristen brought Bailey in. The object of the activity was to have Bailey walk in, turn around and face Kristen, get rewarded for it, and leave. They did exactly that, twice. Both dogs were able to handle it without barking despite the stress of the last time they were in this situation!

We then switched and had Bailey in the corner. He had a really hard time of it; Kristen had him lie down and fed him copious amounts of treats to keep him focused on her. When Marie brought Yankee into the room, he was fine and looked at her immediately. Bailey didn't bark at Yankee, although he knew Yankee was there. Bailey was taking treats with a very **hard mouth**. They repeated this entry a second time and were equally successful. Yay for both dogs!

And finally, Tara brought Max back into the room. For this second session, it took Max only three clicks to be able to take food off the floor while being clicked for looking at Tara, and on the fourth click he took food from Tara's hand. We repeated the plan from the first session; whoever Max looked at said his name and tossed a treat. He really made his rounds this time! He looked at me twice, then Kim twice, then me again, then Tara. He actually refused a treat from her at first, but took it on the second offer. Then he looked at Don once, then at Kim six times (and he wagged at her!). When he next looked at me, I asked him to touch my hand, which he did, for a click and treat. He then looked at Tara, who asked him to touch, which he did, then looked at Kim, but wouldn't touch her hand.

Just as this was happening, Marie walked back into the room. Max growled at her (this was a new behavior for him). But then he looked at Tara. Tara rewarded his focus. He looked at Marie again, who said his name and tossed him treats. We ended the session when he took treats from her hand.

It bears saying that in this context, I consider growling to be a good thing for Max. He shuts down so easily from a lack of confidence that growling indicates an increase in confidence for him. This is not to say that we want a growling dog! We do want him to interact more with people in a positive way, focus more on his owners and communicate his discomfort. The growl told Tara that he was uncomfortable, but his quick focus on her afterward showed that he is beginning to trust Tara more. If she shows him that she is not bothered by the object of the growl, he is more likely to explore it, which he did with Marie. Great way to end the session!

October Fifth

Present: Kim, Don, and Mollie; Deb and Elvis; Kristen, Linda and Bailey; Marie and Yankee; Patti, Tara and Max.

Tonight we started out by noticing that all the dogs seem to be a bit silly, and it's a full moon!

Kim and Deb wanted to do some calming curves together, so we had them start about 80 feet away from each other. This seems to be a recurring distance we use; it has no importance other than it allows the dogs to warm up and get used to what they are doing before we get too close. They first took three steps toward each other, and Mollie barked and looked immediately back at Kim. Kim put her back in the car, as she seemed to be experiencing general arousal, not directed at anyone in particular.

Several minutes later we began again and went five steps. Mollie "boof"ed but did not bark, and Elvis was fine; even with Mollie's barking and boofing he was able to pay attention to Deb. We continued with seven steps and Mollie barked again, so she went back into the car again. (Darn full moon!) Elvis was again able to pay attention through Mollie's barking, but Deb reported that he did have a hard mouth. So we ended their session and will get them out again for another round of something.

Linda and Marie also wanted to do calming curves. We started at 80 feet apart. Linda does not often handle Bailey, but Kristen was out of town and she and Bailey had to get used to working on this exercise together. They each walked three steps toward each other and neither dog barked, but Bailey had almost no focus on Linda at all. We then did four steps and had the same result. I gave Linda a few pointers, such as, "Call your dog as you are about to pivot on your turning foot," and "Turn your shoulders as if you are actually turning, and wait for your dog to come along with you." This improved their teamwork significantly and they did better after that. We repeated four steps again, and Yankee was quicker to turn away from Bailey as well. We repeated four steps yet again, and both dogs did great! At five steps, Yankee continued to do well but Bailey was sniffing around. We repeated five steps again, and this time Bailey gave Yankee a good hard stare, but did not bark, growl, or lunge. So we did five steps again and both dogs did wonderfully, so we ended on a good note.

Kim and Deb had another opportunity to work on calming curves, so we repeated the first session, starting with five steps. Both dogs we able to move with their handlers, pay attention to them, turn when they turned and had little trouble with the concept that another dog was walking toward him/her. We repeated this with six steps, eight steps, ten steps, and then 12 steps. At this point, Mollie started to sniff the ground, so her attention waned, but Elvis continued to do fine. *See Photo 10-05a.* Upon repeating 12 steps, Deb said something to Kim which caused Mollie to bark one time, but was able to stay focused, as was Elvis. And they continued to be successful with 13, 14, and 15 steps! Boy, were those dogs close! Great job!

Linda and Marie also had a chance to do more calming curves, as the first sessions were very short. Again, we started them at five steps. Bailey pulled hard toward Yankee, and Yankee had a hard mouth because of it. So we tried

Photo 10-05a. Mollie's attention wanes during calming curves and she starts sniffing the ground.

five steps again, and both were better. This seemed to be a tough distance for both dogs. At six steps, Bailey pulled hard again and continued to do this on a repeat of six steps. Yankee was able to hold it together and did very well with both repetitions. For some reason, I decided that Marie should do seven steps but Linda should do six steps, and Bailey was better with this. Both dogs were fine and paying attention. Just to be sure, we repeated that level and then had both dogs do seven steps. Bailey did very well with this, and Yankee checked in with Marie on his own! Bailey turned more quickly to go with Linda on her turn that time, too. We finished up with eight steps, and everyone was right on target, so they ended with a party!

Now it was Max's turn, and we all moved into the training room. Max came in with Patti. He needed to check in with Patti and get clicked and actually take and consume a treat from Patti before he could go and investigate people. Remember, Max is a very fearful dog; simple movements and even the quietest noise sends him jumping out of his skin. But Max has been doing this activity for a few weeks now, and he is showing real interest and eagerness to get into the room so he can visit with people! *See Photo 10-05b.*

When he came into the room, he found me, Linda, Deb and Marie sitting on the floor. We decided that perhaps we'd be less scary if we weren't towering

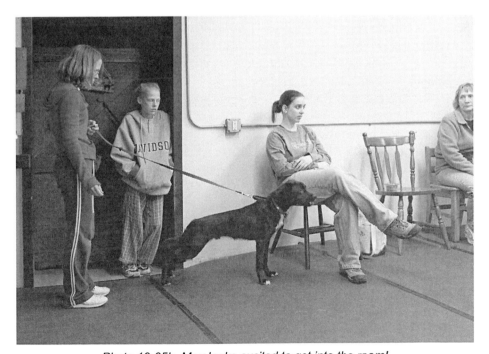

Photo 10-05b. Max looks excited to get into the room!

over him. Tara, Don and Kim were sitting on chairs, just for variety. Max looked at Patti and got clicked three times before he was able to take the treat being offered. Once he was able to take food from Patti, the next time he looked at her, she told him to "go see." He wandered around the room and each time he looked at someone, that person said his name and tossed him a treat. He visited me for two treats, Kim for one, then he went to Tara three times. Then, interestingly enough, he sat in front of Tara and me (I was on the floor and Tara was in a chair next to me) and practically sat on my foot. He then went to Linda one time, Marie twice, Linda once, then Tara, Marie three times, etc. He was very actively scanning the room and looking at people. On average, the treat needed to be tossed about six feet away for him to be comfortable, but occasionally would take a treat from closer, particularly if the person was on the floor or near Tara.

Then he started balking, sat in front of me again and allowed me to pet his entire back, top to bottom. I was very surprised by this! My students often jokingly laugh at me and say, "All dogs love Ali!" (a tease imposed on me by a previous student), but I did not expect this! Dogs are often more comfortable with me than the other people in the room, but this is because I have met with the dog in private lessons for at least three sessions and have spent much time feeding them! For many dogs, I am the first person outside the household that the dog learns to trust. This is particularly the case with Mollie; according to Mollie, I hung the moon. In Max's case, though, I was sitting next to *his* human, Tara. Tara, you may remember, was the person who coined the term, **subsidence** to refer to just this phenomenon.

Don suggested that Patti drop Max's leash. I didn't have time to think this through and give the okay before Patti did just that. Since he was confined to a safe room and his fear response is to run to Tara, it turned out to be fine and in fact, helped him to relax. Max is very sensitive to feeling lured, and Patti has a hard time NOT doing this since she wants so badly for him to improve. Dropping the leash removed some of that, "Oh no, I'm being lured!" reticence. Max then was able to get very close to Don and Marie and took treats from Marie's hand after Tara sat next to her. He even began to play bow to Marie! We are starting to see more play bows from him; this is a conflict behavior for him. He wants to interact, but is so unsure of himself that he is using it as an appeasement behavior. He's very interesting to watch! We also noticed that his flinch response had much diminished by the end of the session; people could move around more in their seats and make some noises, and he didn't go through the roof. Yay for Max!

At this point, I described a new activity for everyone that I thought they'd love. My good friend, **Leslie McDevitt**, came up with this game and showed it to me in a class I've been taking with my own dog, Bing. The name of the game is "Look at That," and it's outlined in detail in Leslie's book, *Control Unleashed: From Stress to Confidence, From Distraction to Focus*. Everyone was interested in it and wanted to try it.

Here's how we did it. All of the humans were in the training room, scattered around. I was sitting in the back of the room with Acacia. The length of the room is about 35 feet, so this is not a big distance. One at a time, each student brings her dog into the room. They were instructed to use their loose leash walking techniques to get from the car to the room in order to maintain the dog's ability to think.** This includes having the dog sit at the door to the room, wait for the owner to open the door, and wait for the cue to go in. The moment the dog goes into the room and sets eyes on Acacia, the owner is to click the dog. Because all of these dogs are very clicker savvy, this is an easy thing for them to do. For the most part, the dogs all turned toward the owner pretty quickly (within three seconds) to get their earned treat.

For two of the four dogs who did this activity (Max did not do this one), their immediate response to seeing Acacia was to bark. The owners simply took the dog outside the door and got some focus, then came back in. In both situations, the dog was much better able to turn his head in response to the click to get the treat. The timing of the click needs to be immediate and simultaneous to the dog seeing Acacia and preferably before the dog starts barking. In each case, within ten clicks, the dog was no longer facing Acacia but was facing his owner, looking over his shoulder at Acacia, getting immediately clicked, looking back at his owner, and getting treated. Once this starts to happen with some consistency, the owner can label this behavior, "Look at that," as in, "Look at that dog." Some of the students called it, "Where's the dog?" By the end of each dog's session, each dog was beginning to understand the concept of, "Where's the dog?" meaning to look at the other dog and get clicked for it.

Leslie puts it this way: If your dog has a problem with a stimulus, make a game out of it. This is exactly what she's done with this activity, and when this behavior is well-trained, the dog's head-turn is incredibly fast. The dog would much rather check back in to the owner for the treat than look at that stupid dog, anyway! I believe that there is some of the **Premack principle**

** Most of the time, dogs are so excited to get into the room that they overreact to all sorts of stimuli. Virtually none of my students will practice loose leash walking with their dogs unless directly instructed to do so, but they all express satisfaction when they follow through with the direction!

going on here, too, with a twist. The higher probability behavior is to look at/bark at the dog, and the lower probability behavior is to look at the owner. By rewarding the earliest stage of noticing the high probability stimulus, the dog is able to turn away from that stimulus to get the treat (lower probability stimulus of looking at owner is inherent in this). Through repetition, the dog finds the focus on the owner to be a better bet – because looking at the owner gets the click and treat – than looking at the dog, because at that point the dog is **subthreshold**. (Whew! Now read that paragraph three more times!)

We were concerned that Mollie might have a really hard time with this since she has decided that she does not like the clicker. Kim made sure to practice using her verbal marker consistently a few times before coming into the room ("Yay!"), and she did just fine.

October Twelfth

Present: Mark and Yankee; Kim, Don, DJ and Mollie; Debbie and Elvis; Kristen, Linda and Bailey; Tara, Patti and Max.

Lately, everyone seems to be enjoying the calming curves, so we continued with it. Mark was at class without Marie, and he is not accustomed to working with Yankee in class, so it was a bit tougher for both him and Yankee. They and Kim and Mollie started with the calming curves from a distance of about 70 feet. When they did three steps, and also four steps, Yankee was in La-La land...looking around and not really paying attention to Mark or to where he was going. He improved on five steps (Mollie did well each time), but on six steps Mollie barked. We repeated six steps, but had them say hello to each other; both dogs tolerated this well. They continued to be fine for seven steps, but on eight steps Yankee started whining, which is an indication that the exercise was becoming difficult for him. We repeated eight steps and they were both okay. On nine steps, Yankee was air sniffing, and he continued to do this for ten steps. Since the dogs were rather close to each other at this time (about 12 feet), we stopped there before it became so difficult for Yankee that he felt he had to bark.

Since Kristen was late due to traffic and we wanted to take advantage of the quickly disappearing sunlight, Debbie got Elvis out of the car and planned to walk him near the folks gathered near the barn. Sometimes Elvis can be reactive to people, but Debbie doesn't usually work on this issue because dogs are more of an issue for Elvis, and she wants to run him in agility. He started out doing okay, paying attention to Debbie, but Kristen and Bailey came walking around the corner and he began to bark at them. So, back in the car they went.

As it turns out, we made a mistake; Bailey needed more time to calm down. He had been home all day long and then barely had a walk before he got into the car for an hour's drive. He had a very difficult time staying focused.

Here's what happened:

They started from 60 feet away and walked three steps toward each other. They were both okay with this, and were even more focused on four and then five steps. On six steps, Bailey was walking on his back feet, but was not barking. About this time, Elvis got stepped on, screeched and then decided that while he was at it, he might as well bark at Bailey, so back in the car they both went.

At this time, we all went into the training room. Patti brought Max in and waited for him to look at her so she could click and offer him a treat. He looked at her eight times and got clicked, but didn't want the treat…he wanted to go visit people! It just so happened that we were sitting in a rather tight circle and he felt very constricted. We realized this too late to do much about it at the time; any big movements would have sent him running. So one by one, we turned in different directions so as not to all be looking straight at him. This helped only minimally, and he continued to have a difficult time giving eye contact to any one person. We ended his session and talked about what to do differently for his next session.

We did a repeat of the "Look at that" exercise from last week. Each dog did a tremendous job of looking and turning away from the dog. Since Mark wasn't used to working with Yankee in the class, he fumbled a bit but did very well, and within about four clicks, he sat with his back to Bing. Bing is my 1½ year old intact male Belgian Sheepdog, who is VERY dog friendly and also very active, and was my demo dog for the evening. Yankee exhibits some very obvious anxious behaviors when another dog is around. He has learned to not look at the dog but to check in with his person. He has learned this lesson well! He did not stare at Bing, but only took a quick glance at him then checked back in with Mark for confirmation.

Kristen, who had not been at class the previous week, didn't think that Bailey could do it! At first, he came into the room and immediately barked at Bing. But once he left the room, gathered his wits and re-entered, he was able to compose himself enough to lie down in front of Kristen and look over at Bing. It took him longer than it took with Acacia, but he knows Bing less well from class than he knows Acacia, and he had worked with another handler the previous week.

Elvis had a substantially more difficult time with this activity. Debbie had warned us that he was having a tough day. He came in and spent quite a bit of time barking at Bing. His response was very variable; about 50% of the time he'd look at Bing and check right back in to Debbie. The rest of the time he spent huffing and barking and making himself loud and important. At one point, he even pulled the leash out of Debbie's hand, came running over to Bing, stopped about two feet in front of him, threw his weight onto his back legs and growl/barked. He was clearly unsure of what to do! To me, this is the quintessential reactive dog – all bluff and very little action. Debbie called him and Elvis came running back to her. We all made sure she rewarded him lots for coming back to her! I asked her to get in a few more clicks and end on a good note. Elvis was certainly having a rough night, and after all that barking, I didn't think he'd learn any more.

Mollie did well again despite Kim using a verbal marker instead of a clicker (I think the clicker is immensely useful for this activity because it is so immediate), and despite my clicking for Bing. Mollie's demeanor changed when she started to look at Bing; her ears went floppy, she hunched her back a bit, she moved slowly. It was clear that the situation was stressful for her. After a few minutes of her looking at Bing, Don wondered out loud how Mollie would get along with Bing. Mollie, of late, has been quite the social butterfly. I agreed to let them interact. Bing ran right up to her (on leash) and she simply allowed him to sniff. I was concerned that Bing might try his favorite stunt on Mollie (the hump!) but he didn't. They sniffed noses and both dogs seemed to be fine. We talked briefly about having Mollie come early one night to play with Bing.

The second session with Max was very unorthodox! I realized almost too late that I needed to get rid of Bing for his session, since his session was all about becoming brave enough to interact with people. But we all looked at each other, and knowing that Max likes other dogs, we decided to keep Bing in the room. Max made a beeline toward Bing, and they played for a while. Max did much hopping around and play bowing, which is lovely to see. He was hesitant to take food from others, but Bing wasn't. Each time Bing went to a new person, Max tried to engage him in play. Eventually, Max noticed that Bing was getting attention and treats, and he followed suit. Subsidence! Yay for Max!

October Nineteenth

Present: Kim, Don and Mollie; Kristen, Linda and Bailey; Marie, Mark and Yankee; Deb and Elvis; Patti, Tara and Max.

Everyone continues to enjoy doing the calming curves with their dogs because it simulates the sort of thing they often have trouble with on walks.

Kim and Marie did some calming curves with Mollie and Yankee. They started 85 feet apart and began with four steps. At this distance, both dogs were fine. I usually start with this simple distance just to help everyone warm up. At five steps, Yankee whined and Mollie barked. We repeated five steps. Clearly they were not ready to continue, and Mollie barked again. Most of Mollie's barking is now a general excitement bark rather than a reactive "There's a dog!" bark. So, we repeated five steps again and both dogs were fine. It is important to note that while Mollie is barking, Yankee is managing to hold it together! We moved up to seven steps, and Yankee looked at Mollie for a full three seconds but was able to continue working. At eight steps, Marie reported that Yankee's mouth was really hard. But at ten steps, Yankee was still able to work, while Mollie turned back and barked at Yankee after they turned away from each other. At 11 steps, Mollie "boof"ed, and Yankee continued to have a hard mouth.

Because we continued to see this trend with Mollie, we stopped and questioned the function of the barking behavior. We came up with a new plan: when Mollie barks, Marie will make sure that Yankee does not go away, but Kim calls Mollie front. Yankee would continue to do as many steps as was predetermined. We began to suspect that Mollie was barking to get Kim to take her away from Yankee. We did 12 steps, and Mollie "boof"ed at 11½ steps and immediately checked back in with Kim just as they were about to turn anyway! We stopped there for that session, so we didn't really need to enact our new plan.

Debbie wanted to just spend some time with Elvis on attention while another dog was around. We decided to use Bing. She got Elvis out of the car while Bing was about 50 feet away. We were both doing typical focus exercises such as hand targeting, sit, down, sit at heel, spin, bow, etc. Debbie moved around within a small radius while I walked around a larger boundary area, then gradually came in to about 40 feet. Elvis made this look easy, although he was watchful of what we were doing. After about three minutes, I backed away to about 50 feet and Debbie moved toward me with Elvis, working him closer for a brief time, then backing away to take off some pressure. We ended up working our dogs within about 30 feet and Elvis appeared to be doing okay, but the session was too long for him. Bing looked at Elvis straight on, Elvis barked and that was the end of the session. Direct eye contact, particularly from a male, is too challenging for Elvis at this time.

Kristen was really excited because after over 1 ½ years of work, I FINALLY said that Bailey was ready to "work the room!" *See Photos 10-19a through 10-19f.* We began by having everyone in the training room while I stood near the door and waited for him to come in and pay attention to Kristen so we could do a send-off. The purpose of this was first, for Bailey to focus on his owner, and second, to greet a more familiar person before meeting less known people. Everyone else was sitting around the room, holding out a treat in their hands. He happily went around the room, munching treats from Kim, Don, Tara, Deb, Mark, Marie and Linda. He did this perfectly and went around the room a second time with no barking, no staring, and no intense sniffing! (At one time, intense sniffing of a person was a clear antecedent to looking up and letting out his incredibly scary bark.) They ran out of the room and had a HUGE party!!!

Patti then got Max while the rest of us sat in a circle of chairs around a small table in the far corner of the room. (We were eating birthday treats!) Patti and Tara expressed frustration at Max's complete lack of focus on them while on a walk, and now, in the room with them because he is so interested in visiting with the people. What a change from only a few weeks ago, when Max wanted nothing to do with strangers! So the plan here was for us to be unobtrusive while they worked near the entrance to the room. Patti brought Max in and waited for him to look at her. He looked at her six times for six clicks, and only ate half the treats; the rest were on the floor. I had instructed Patti to offer a treat even if he doesn't take it. He could take the treat later if he wanted. During this time, one ten-second interval passed during which Max paid Patti no attention, so she took him out into the lobby until he was able to focus.

She then brought him in again and clicked him 12 times for looking at her.

a

b

c

Photos 10-19a through 10-19f. Send-offs: (a) Bailey sits and looks at Kristen. (b) Kristen points toward the visitor, takes a step forward and says, "Go see." At the same time, the visitor holds out a pointer finger and says, "Here." Bailey finger targets. (c) Bailey then sits for treats in front of visitor. (d) When the visitor is finished greeting the dog, she points back to Kristen, saying, "Go see." At the same time, Kristen asks Bailey for a finger target. (e) Bailey happily turns his back on the visitor and sits in front of Kristen for treats. (f) The process is repeated. Note Bailey's open mouth and very happy smile.

On that last click, she treated him and ran out of the room to celebrate. They came back in and did about another 12 clicks and treats. By now he was eating the treats. On the last click, she dropped the leash and let him come over to us. This seemed to be the biggest reward for him! He was so interested in us that it seemed only fair that if he worked for Patti, he should be able to visit with his new friends. He moved around the outside of the circle and took treats from those people's hands that were close enough for him to get to. Everyone kept their faces toward the middle of the circle, so Max didn't have to make direct eye contact. Coming into the middle of the circle was entirely too difficult for him. We are going to call this "schmoozing the crowd" or "working the room." After about five minutes of this, Patti took him out for a break.

Mollie and Yankee wanted to do some more calming curves. This time we started with five steps because they'd warmed up earlier. Five steps are easy for them now. At seven steps, Mollie let out a little growl and Yankee air-sniffed. Both dogs repeated these behaviors for eight steps, and then Yankee peed. After that, both dogs did great…at 8, 10, 12 and 14 steps. At 14 steps, Marie was nervous but the dogs were fine! At the apex, the dogs were 12 feet away from each other, head to head.

We decided to switch the game since both dogs were doing well with this and because both dogs seemed to want to visit the people standing near the garage. The new game was "Where's the dog?" and Yankee started it while Mollie visited the people. Mollie almost immediately barked at Mark, who lifted his arm to reach into this pocket for a treat. She returned to her car. Yankee then schmoozed the crowd (sat for treats from everyone) while Mollie, after a few minutes, came out of the car and worked on "Where's the dog?" They then switched and Mollie visited with people for treats while Yankee worked on "Where's the dog?" Both dogs did fine with this exercise.

Elvis repeated his work from the first session but this time he worked opposite Acacia. The pattern of movement on our parts was pretty much the same, and Elvis did fine. He seems to have a more difficult time with male dogs (both he and Bing are intact). The main difference in this session is that Acacia came closer, to about 25 feet. At this point, we both stayed more or less stationary and worked on "Where's the Dog?" Elvis did great; he had a quick head turn from Deb to the dog and back to Deb again.

Because it was such a nice night, we decided to do Bailey's session of "schmooze the crowd" outside in the garage. Again, we started with me doing a send-off with him. This was followed by him going around to each person and taking a treat from an outstretched hand. Bailey had to deal with standing people this time instead of sitting people, and despite this, he did great! His behavior was perfect, his eyes were calm and happy, his ears and tail relaxed, and he didn't bark at anyone.

For Max's second session, we repeated the first session but he worked with Tara. Usually he does better with Tara, whether it's because it's his second attempt or because he is more attached or in tune with Tara, I don't know. But tonight he was worse during his second session. He gave less focus than in the first session. After ten seconds of a complete lack of focus and whining to get to the people, Tara took him out into the lobby for 20 seconds and completely ignored him (negative punishment), then brought him back in. This seemed to help greatly. He did some sits, touches, finger targets and other skills for about 12 clicks, then Tara told him to "go see!" and dropped his leash. He ran over to the circle of people sitting in the corner of the room and went around, eating treats out of the outstretched hands of the people closest to him. It took him quite a while to decide that it was okay to take food from peoples' hands, but he did so.

October Twenty-Seventh

Present: Kim, Don and Mollie; Marie, Mark and Yankee; Linda and Bailey; Patti, Tara and Max; Deb and Elvis.

Tonight, Marie and Linda did some calming curves with a twist: one dog walked straight and the other came around a corner toward the first one. They switched places so both dogs had the opportunity to be in both situations. *See Illustration 10-27a.*

We started with three steps, meaning that Yankee walked straight without counting while Bailey turned the corner and then Linda counted three steps. Both dogs remained quiet but Bailey had little focus. With four steps, Bailey was staring (and wagging and looking around at the people he wanted to get food from!) and had no focus on Linda, but had a happy look on his face. Linda decided to put him back in the car. I thought this was a wise decision. She waited for about two minutes, then brought him out of the car again, and this time, with five steps around the corner, he was able to pay much better attention. Yankee was a bit hard-mouthed but remained focused on Marie.

We then switched and had Bailey walk straight while Yankee came around the corner and Marie counted one step. Both dogs remained quiet (Linda was practicing "Where's the dog?"). With two steps, Yankee did okay but turned wide, indicating to me that he wasn't really paying close attention to Marie. Attention, in general, increased with three steps, as the dogs seemed to be figuring out the game, and with four steps both dogs seemed to be happy. However, on five steps, while Linda was waiting for Yankee to come, she was in the process of sitting on the ground when Bailey saw Yankee come. Given the slightest opportunity, he lunged at Yankee, pulling Linda off the ground. We discussed the importance of putting him immediately back in the car for this behavior; it is important for a dog as large and as strong as Bailey to not only not lunge at other dogs but to learn to check in when he sees a dog. Bailey

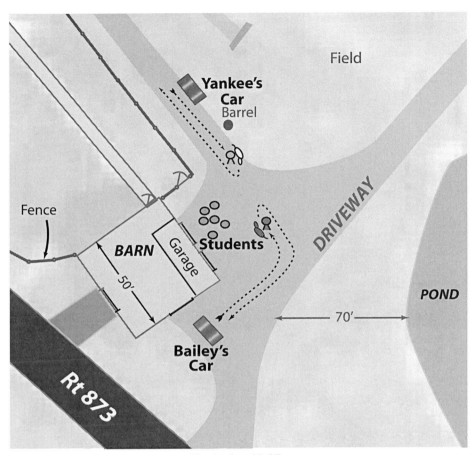

Illustration 10-27a.

still has not learned that his owners have the responsibility of taking care of these extraneous stimuli; he still acts as if it's his job to "get" to the other dog or person.

After a short car break for Bailey (three minutes) we resumed this activity, and Bailey's attention was suddenly impeccable. The dogs went six steps around the corner and were able to come within 20 feet of each other without reacting.

We did some CGC greetings with Mollie in the training room. *See Photo 10-27b.* Mollie was sitting next to Kim, and I stood about ten feet away from them. Each time Mollie looked at Kim, Kim marked the behavior and I took a step closer to them. When I was about five feet away from them, Mollie grunted several times at me because I was standing still. For many dogs, a person who suddenly acts differently than how they normally act will be cause

Photo 10-27b. Mollie and Kim are practicing CGC greetings with Kristen doing the greeting (photo taken prior to this session's writing).

for alarm. To Mollie, I am never standing still! The rest of the greeting went without a hitch. Deb also did the same exercise with Mollie. Mollie is not all that familiar with Deb, but she was able to do this very well, with no barking or grunting. Deb even gave Mollie treats while bending over her!

Patti had a turn at greeting Mollie. She started at ten feet, but when she got to four feet, Mollie barked. Patti started walking away, but I asked her to go back to where she was standing when Mollie barked and continue, which she did. She was able to get close enough to treat Mollie without having her bark, but Mollie's mouth was hard and she had to stand up (she was unable to remain seated).

For Max's session we all sat in the middle of the room facing each other, and had treats in our hands which we held out behind us. When Max initially came into the room, Patti only had to wait about one minute for Max to be able to look at her and take a treat from her! This is a big improvement over just a few weeks ago when it took several minutes for him to be calm enough to even look at Patti! Max then "schmoozed the crowd" (after checking in with Patti) and went around eating treats from peoples' hands. He ate from everyone's hands. At this time he was off leash. After a few minutes of this, Patti put his leash back on and walked him around the room and directed him to take treats.

He did fine until he felt tension on the leash; at that time, he dug in his heels and wouldn't move. The leash is definitely a barrier for him.

Elvis and Acacia did some calming curves. We started at about 75 feet away from each other and gradually got closer. Elvis looked great, gave Deb wonderful focus, and didn't bark at all. He had a hard mouth at 11 steps, so we repeated that step and his mouth was a bit softer the second time. Deb reported that her cleaning ladies inadvertently let Elvis out of the house this afternoon and he went wandering around the neighborhood. He wasn't gone long and no harm came to him, but his entire demeanor was better tonight! (This is NOT the recommended treatment for reactive dogs, by the way!)

For Yankee's second session, Marie worked for about six minutes on "Where's the dog?" with Acacia at the other end of the room. It was immediately clear that he had a very difficult time looking at Acacia; he had learned so well to NOT look at another dog that now looking at one was stressful for him. Instead, he spent much time looking at the other people in the room. After several minutes of this, he relaxed visibly, laid down, looked at Acacia and looked back at Marie and wagged his tail. What an improvement in a short time!

Bailey also did "Where's the dog?" but we changed his program a bit. Linda was instructed to bring him in, and the second he looked at Acacia, she was to click and treat and take him back out. She repeated this a second time, and the third time she remained in the room after she clicked him for looking at her. Within only a few seconds, he laid down and began to offer Linda other behaviors, such as showing his tummy. After about two minutes of this, I had Acacia begin to move around more; I had had her in a down position, facing away from Bailey. Now Acacia sat, stood and jumped up to touch my hand. With all of this, Bailey was able to remain calm and look at her and back to Linda. But then Acacia looked at Bailey, and that was too much; she stared at him and he stared back. Linda was talking to us and missed her click; as a result, he barked and she had to take him out of the room.

For Mollie's turn at this skill, she immediately barked upon coming into the room (old habits die hard, I think). It was suggested that someone other than me handle Acacia so I handed the leash off to Linda, whom Acacia knows well. Mollie had gone out of the room, so when she came back in, I was not handling Acacia. Mollie did much better with the second entry. As her focus on Acacia and back to Kim increased in speed, everyone in the room said, "Yay!" Mollie seemed to thrive on this. There was a time, not long ago, when that sort of noise would have sent her curling into a tiny ball. It's so lovely to see this new Mollie!

Elvis also had a turn at "Where's the puppy?' with Acacia. He again did wonderfully during his session. We broke up the entry for him as well…he came in, got one click and treat for looking at her (it took him about 20 seconds to actually look at her), went out into the lobby, then came back in for two clicks, went out, then came back in again for two more clicks, went out, then came back in and Deb sat in a chair while they worked on the activity. Asking the dogs to look at the "scary" thing and then taking the pressure off of them a few times – by taking them out of the room – seems to really help them to be able to handle the situation much more effectively.

After Acacia left, Max came in and cruised the circuit again. This time he came in with Tara, took less than one minute to focus on her AND take a treat. He was whining to get to the people, though, for at least three minutes. Tara then let him off the leash and he went around to everyone and continued to take food from them. Max had the most difficult time with men, but was able to take food from all of them. He also went in the middle of the circle to take food, and went under the small table in the middle of the circle for food treats which had rolled under there. What a brave dog!

December Seventh

Present: Kim and Mollie; Deb and Elvis; Patti, Tara and Max; Linda, Kristen and Bailey

It's been so long since we had class – due to holidays, my absence and my illness – that I decided that it would be to everyone's benefit to simply begin at the beginning. It is typical for dogs to experience regression in the absence of practice to "keep the gears oiled," so we wanted to ease back into our work.

Each dog had the opportunity to practice getting out of the car and focusing on the owner, then walking into the lobby, sitting and focusing for several clicks. The humans were each instructed to remain in the lobby until the dog gave calm body language, such as soft eyes, open mouth, sitting, looking at the owner, or letting out a sigh/puff of air. For some dogs, this required upwards of five minutes; most took one to three minutes. The next step was to open the training room door, have the dog wait, then allow him through, calling his name immediately. The owner didn't pass the threshold and gave the dog a full ten seconds to turn around and look at the owner. Once the dog is clicked and treated, they returned to the lobby, regained focus out there, and repeated the process of opening the door and crossing the threshold. This process was completed three times per dog. Those of us who were watching really enjoyed the increased speed with which each dog focused over the three repetitions. It was a validating experience to see the power of this activity, a great reminder of how much our dogs have learned, and the importance of focus. The biggest problem we had was with sniffing the entrance way; none of the dogs barked or otherwise reacted.

The second round of work included everything from the first round, and then if the dog was showing calmness while focusing when coming into the room, the owner would sit in a chair near the door. Some dogs needed to go back out to the lobby once, some twice. We were all pleasantly surprised by how well the dogs were all able to focus on the owners at this stage. The duration of sitting in the chair was brief the first time (about ten seconds), and then they returned to the lobby, got focus, and came back in again, sat down a second and third time.

These first two rounds went very quickly and very well. As it turned out, we had time for a third session. Each owner selected a new distraction for the dog for this third round. Everyone but Patti and Tara decided to have people walk around. We choreographed who would move to where so that there would be purpose in action with no hesitation. The only dog who barked was Bailey, when Kim came out of the restroom, which was unplanned. All Kristen did was take Bailey out to the lobby to refocus. When they came back in he was much improved. Again, we enjoyed watching (over a period of only a few minutes) Kristen ask for each behavior, often just as he was orienting toward someone or a sound, to letting him look at the person and then calling him back, to just letting him check in with her on his own. He also offered lots of lying down and relaxing.

It is interesting to note that Elvis and Mollie clearly were excited to return to school. Elvis only wanted to come and visit me, wagging his stumpy tail furiously. Mollie was permitted to visit with each person for treats as her reward for paying such lovely attention.

But it is Max who deserves the most attention in this log entry! Up until now, my work with Max has been rather free-form. Once his family completed their individual lessons and joined the group, there was very little operant conditioning and mostly classical conditioning happening. Max's behavior is almost exclusively fear-based; reactivity is close to nonexistent. Our major goal has been to reduce the flight response toward people, so we'd been giving him tons of opportunity to associate people with good things. Patti, in particular, found this process to be quite disheartening and very frustrating. She was afraid he'd never "get better." I'm sure there were times when she nearly decided to not return to class.

It all paid off tonight!

We had not really spent much time asking Max to focus on Patti or Tara or Glen. When we did ask him to pay attention to them, it was to gain access to some immediate reward, such as the opportunity to move closer to the people or get treats from them. And then, too, focus was brief. Tonight, we had Max do exactly what the other dogs were doing. This was a first! It took Max and Patti at least five minutes in the lobby to become calm enough to gain focus. We heard a lot of whining, and not much clicking, but the rate of clicking increased after several minutes. Once he was in the room, I didn't expect him to pay attention to Patti within ten seconds; we just waited. Initially, he gave very cursory attention and Patti clicked and dropped treats on the floor. But after only about three of these, he suddenly started to turn around toward Patti and look straight at her! And then he began to sit and look at her! We were all astonished! This was the first time that Max was calm enough to be able to give this sort of focus...yippee!!

Patti took him out of the room, refocused him in the lobby and repeated the process twice. Once she was able to sit down, I have to admit that I started to hold my breath. But he was fabulous! He just sat and looked at Patti, offered sits and downs, and shakes and spins – total, complete focus on her! After several minutes of this newfound ability to focus, Patti sent him off to visit his friends for treats. He took treats from everyone in the room, even if he had to outstretch his legs every now and again from fear. We all asked Patti who this new dog was and what had happened to Max...but she was wondering the same thing!

Patti did tell us a secret, though. During our long hiatus from class, she miscommunicated and drove to class twice when we didn't have class. Max got all excited to come, despite his dislike of the car, and then had to turn around and go home. Poor Max! We wonder if this didn't have some sort of effect on his ability to pay attention. I always say that absence makes the heart grow fonder, but this took place over the course of a month. I suppose it's a secret we'll never know.

Tara did repeat the process when it was Max's next turn and he did equally well with her. I have seen this frequently with reactive dogs – they seem to dilly-dally along for months and months, and then all of a sudden, it's as if a light bulb goes on and they suddenly reach the next level of ability. Yay for Max! As we were wrapping up for the night, Tara noticed that there were no men present tonight and wondered if this could have contributed to his success, since he does seem to be more afraid of men.

December Fourteenth

Present: Kim, Don and Mollie; Linda and Bailey; Marie, Mark and Yankee; Tara, Patti and Max. Observers: Christie and Pat.

Tonight's class was intended to be more or less a repeat of last week's class. The differences were that we had men present tonight and we had Yankee but not Elvis.

We began our rounds with the same protocol as last week and everyone did very well. We had the dogs come into the lobby, focus on the owner, come into the training room, focus on the owner, have the owner sit down and keep the dog's attention without needing to react. We did this for one round per dog. Sometimes a review such as this is very beneficial.

Yankee's second round involved having me bring Bing out of the house and walk toward the barn while having him focus on Marie. We did this for about five minutes, and Yankee's behavior told us that he was studiously ignoring Bing. Yay for Yankee! At one point, Marie told me that his mouth was hard, so I backed Bing off by about ten feet and Yankee was much better. This told us that he was very aware of Bing's presence and was remembering to not react.

Bailey's second round involved people walking around in the room. Bailey is always very interested in what's going on around him, and often feels the need to "object" to something that's happening. Tonight, he managed to look at the commotion and turn back to Linda with no barking whatsoever. It was all fairly low level activity; we were walking around the room, one person at a time, each having a "job" to do. In the past, this would not have been possible at all. We basically were reconfirming that Bailey was able to manage himself in this type of distraction. What a lovely reminder.

Kim wanted to have Mollie interact with Bing. She brought Mollie into the room while I had Bing at the far end of the room. Bing's focus on me isn't nearly as good as Acacia's, and he was missing his playtimes with other dogs since I had been away. This created a very distracting situation for Mollie, but she held it together. She did not even "boof" at Bing! She spent a fair amount of time looking around, but was able to return her gaze to Kim with little trouble. After several minutes of this, Kim let Mollie's leash go, and she came over to Bing. I let his leash drag, too, and they interacted very appropriately. Bing seemed slightly more interested in her than she was in him, but there was no trouble, no stillness, and no fear. It didn't take long for them to begin to ignore each other in favor of "working the room for treats." They went around the room, sitting for treats, sometimes together, sometimes at different parts of the room. What fun!

We ended the evening by having Tara and Max do more or less the same thing. The difference with Max was that he really loves to play with dogs, so he and Bing were playing a lot more than Mollie and Bing had been. At one point I had to go over and take off Bing's leash because I was afraid it would tangle. As I approached Max (they were playing), he urinated quite a lot, but this did not stop him from continuing his game. We still have much to work on with Max, but any progress worth making is slow. Max and Bing seemed much less inclined to "work the room," so we started to call Bing to us, each in turn, for treats. The intent was to have Bing demonstrate for Max the benefit of visiting with people. We used Bing as a tool for **subsidence**.

Max was a bit more hesitant overall tonight compared to last week when it came to taking treats, but he did take treats from everyone's hands, including all of the men and the new people! I think we were all heaving sighs of relief that Max's performance last week wasn't an anomaly!

Sadly, Max will be kenneled for the next two weeks. We are hopeful that he will maintain his newfound success in class. Patti mentioned that he is much less fearful of people in the park these days. If he sees a person with a dog, he is much more likely to just march up to them, and care little about the person attached to the dog. Progress!!

December Twenty-First and Twenty-Eighth

During these classes, we continued with similar activities, but I did not take notes, as we used some of our class time for holiday parties. The beauty of this class is that the humans learn much about each other, share jokes, books, DVDs, and other items of interest. During this time, we shared wine, beer, cookies, candy, cake, and a host of other goodies, including champagne for New Year's! Also, between Christmas and New Year's, we expanded the training room by tearing out walls, removing an interior garage door and building an outside wall with a door in the place of the exterior garage door. To see what the training room looks like now *see Illustration 12-21a.* This not only increased our usable space, but it also provided us with two entrances/exits. The implications for reactive class will be tremendous! My original intent was to stop taking notes of class for this book at the end of the year; however, I realized that I could demonstrate other activities for reactive dog class if I took notes for a few more weeks. So now, you get a few bonus weeks to read!

Max was away for these two weeks, so he was not in attendance. However, Shadow began his classes with Christi. She was very worried that he would just bark the entire time so she was a bit nervous to begin. Most new students have this same concern. His first session began on the 28th, and he was the very first dog to use the new side door! I had Christi get Shadow out of the car, call his name, click and treat him for looking at her, do a few skills and party in the car. She repeated this twice, and the third time, I had the new door open so he could see inside. The people were all at the other side of the room, but he could see, hear and smell them. I had Christi take one step into the room and call his name. She clicked and treated him, and they left the room. She ended her session there. When it was her turn again, she began with Shadow taking one step into the room. Shadow did very well; she had him sit in the room for about ten seconds, asking him for skills, and he remained beautifully focused until someone stood up. This caused Shadow to bark and ended his session.

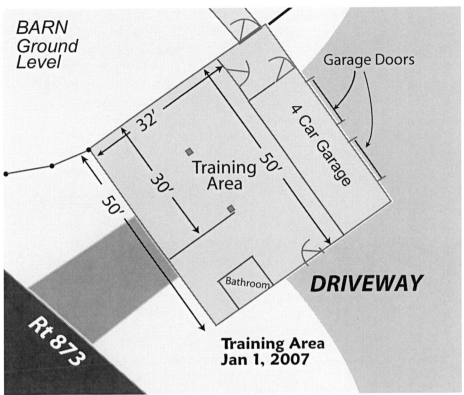

Illustration 12-21a. The main training area was expanded from 32' x 21' to 32' x 30' with a 50' long span. Numerous inside walls and two garage doors were removed. Heat, additional insulation, a new ceiling and an exterior door were added.

Overall, he did great, and both Christi and Pat were shocked.

In the ensuing weeks, Shadow was a quick study, and took on just about every distraction we threw at him. During January, another new student team joined us; Lisa and Indy. For a variety of reasons, Indy only made it to one class in January, but her introduction was similar to Shadow's. She progressed even more quickly than Shadow because her trigger is dogs, not people. Indy was able to come into the room for her first session and sit, calmly focusing on Lisa, while the humans sat and talked. It was important for her to assimilate all of this information before adding the difficult stimulus to the mix. For her second session, I had Acacia lying at the back of the room, facing toward me and away from Indy. Indy was able to ignore Acacia. Lisa was frustrated because she felt that Indy didn't really see Acacia; we all reassured her that Indy was *quite* aware of Acacia's presence, but because Acacia's body language was very nonconfrontational, Indy did not feel the need to defend herself.

When Patti came back to class she reported that while Max apparently did fine at the kennel, he was quite scared of the family when they came to get him. He acted as though he didn't know them and it took him two weeks to return to the dog he was when they dropped him off. Clearly, the stress of being kenneled was overwhelming for him. But his next session went extremely well, despite Patti's fears for the worst. Max really enjoys coming to class, so that may have helped him to resettle.

We actually cancelled class a few times due to inclement weather, so we will fast forward to February.

February First

Present: Marie and Yankee; Kristen, Linda, Steve and Bailey; Deb and Elvis; Kim, Don and Mollie; Patti and Max; Christi and Shadow.

Yankee and Mollie began tonight's session. The humans sat in groupings set up to serve as partial visual barriers between the two doors. As Marie predicted, Yankee came in and tried to "work the crowd" for treats, but we were all very good students and ignored him until he paid attention to Marie. This often becomes a problem with our dogs; we spend so much time rewarding our reactive dogs for interacting with people that they begin to make these decisions for themselves and we end up having to reel them in. Mollie then came in the front door and was immediately wagging at everyone for attention. I asked Kim to go out and try that entry again, but this time, don't actually come into the room. Just stand in the threshold and get her focus. Mollie's response was much improved the second time.

Yankee was very excited to see Mollie (!!!). He whined and let out one little bark and Marie took him around a corner to get his attention back. In response to this, Mollie growled at Yankee, but when Yankee returned, she was able to maintain attention. Yankee, however, distributed his attention between Marie and Mollie, and did TWO PLAY BOWS TO HER!!! None of us could believe our eyes! We all said, "Who are you and what have you done with Yankee?"

Marie took Yankee out the side door while Mollie went over to where Yankee had been. Marie then brought Yankee in the front door. We have been doing this activity quite a bit lately, because being in a room and having a dog enter the room is quite different than coming into a room and seeing another dog in there. It's more difficult to be in a room and have a dog come in to join you, so we have dogs practice both options. Both Mollie and Yankee were able to pay appropriate attention to their people for about four minutes, at which time Yankee's mouth began to get hard. Marie took Yankee out the front door and Kim took Mollie out the side door. After this session, we discussed the possibility of these two greeting each other during the next session.

The next two dogs were Max and Elvis. We decided to do some calming curves into the room, through the doors. Max came in the front door threshold and barely crossed it before Patti turned and called him out. Max had good focus and looked right back at Patti. Elvis came in the side door at the same time, but came farther into the room, to the end of his leash. Deb called him out and tried again, this time calling him sooner as she crossed the threshold. Elvis' focus improved. But Max had a good long look at Elvis, and had a harder time turning around than he did the first time. The third time both dogs came in, they stayed in their entrance ways for about 15 seconds, working for clicks and treats.

This was a very new concept for Max; he has never been asked to pay immediate attention upon coming into the room, much less turn around and go back out. Max still needs to take his time before he is ready to focus (this is part of his fear response), so he was doing a lot of looking around. The fourth time they both came into the room, Elvis caught Max looking at him, and Elvis began barking so Deb took him back to the car. Meanwhile, Patti walked with Max on leash around the room. He walked behind peoples' chairs and took treats from their outstretched hands so he didn't have to approach peoples' faces. He still often plants his back feet and reaches out with his front feet in the classic approach-avoidance posture, but is less tentative about taking the food. *See Photos 2-01a through 2-01c.* Deb came back into the room and walked right past Max, but he didn't back away at all. This is progress! He also walked in between two rows of chairs to get to another person for a treat, but instead of walking all the way through, he stopped and backed up. Again, this is significant improvement for him.

Next, Bailey and Shadow practiced calming curves into the room at the same time, using the different doors. They just go at their own pace, and the dogs see different doggy body parts as they do this. Sometimes they see a tail, sometimes a face, sometimes the side of a body. Bailey had good focus the third time he came in, while Shadow was in the lobby. The next time they came in, they saw each others' faces and both started to bark. Kristen and Christi worked with their dogs out of the room until they were able to sustain attention, and then they started their calming curves again. The next time they came in, Shadow immediately looked for Bailey, and took 9.9 seconds to focus on Christi. Who says dogs don't know how to count??? Bailey let out a small "boof" toward Shadow, so he went out of the room again. When they both returned to the room, they were able to ignore each other for a few seconds (finally), so we ended there on a good note.

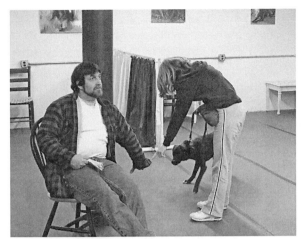

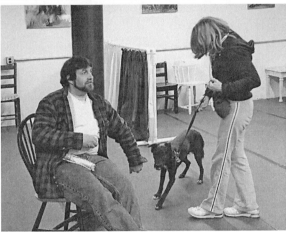

Photo 2-01a through 2-01c. Patti sends Max to see a treat in Don's hand. Max's weight is on his back legs; he is conflicted about whether the treat is worth it. Max takes the treat and beats a hasty retreat.

This particular exercise was very difficult for both dogs. Shadow hadn't done this activity before, and Bailey has a much harder time working with other male dogs than with females. It also addresses the challenge of **sudden environmental contrast**, which is very common in reactive dogs. The concept of sudden contrast involves the perception that something which suddenly appears is out of context. For example, Acacia has always been perfectly behaved at dog shows. She's been shown for years – ever since she was a pup. In her mind, hundreds of dogs in one particular place make sense to her. But put her on a walking trail through the woods and let one dog come around a curve, and she will have a very hard time containing herself. Likewise, for many of these dogs, the idea of a person suddenly appearing in a doorway is enough to make them blow a gasket. Using calming curves into the room teaches the dogs new muscle memory and the thought process of, "I see something strange which makes me uncomfortable, so I must check in with my person."

Yankee and Mollie's second round involved coming into the room separately, from different doors, and doing **send-offs** to a group of people. Each dog had a group of three seated people to visit. Kim sent Mollie right to Don successfully, but Yankee was distracted by sniffing people, so Marie had to take him out to regain focus. While Mollie was visiting with Don, he stood up as he was feeding her. Mollie had no reaction. Yankee came back in, and was still spotty with his focus, but was able to go visit Steve, who stood up to do the send-off. Yankee had no trouble with this (Yankee is not people reactive). Kim sent Mollie off to visit with Patti, who followed Don's lead and stood up as she was feeding her. Mollie still had no trouble. Deb stood up and Marie sent Yankee to her. He was calm and happy. So each dog had the opportunity to visit with the people in his or her group and then go back to the handler.

When this was done, I explained what we would do to have the dogs greet each other. They started about 15 feet away from each other, got their dogs' focus, then took a step toward each other, pointed at the other dog, and said, "Go see." I counted three seconds, at which time each person called her dog away to focus back on them. It was really beautiful to see! They wagged and sniffed each other's flews. Their body language appeared to be quite relaxed! Everyone was so excited that the second time they did this, Yankee was all wound up and pawed at Mollie, Mollie pawed back, and both dogs' behavior accelerated very quickly, so we called them away. After giving them about a minute to relax, the handlers sent their dogs much more slowly. Yankee initially lunged forward so Marie called him back. The final attempt to greet each other lasted only two seconds, but it was friendly and involved sniffing. Success!

Elvis' second session was a solo one. Deb wanted to have Elvis greet people, so he could learn that people are good. She brought him in the front door and sent him off to each person in turn. Usually we do this using finger targets, but Elvis uses hand targets, so it was confusing to him at first. However, he greeted everyone appropriately, and his only difficulty was that he wanted to sniff Patti. At this point, each person stood up one at a time and moved around the room. Don stood up and walked over to the heater to inspect it, Christi went to look in the toy basket, I walked out the front door and back in again, and each time, Elvis had no trouble with the movement. Don stood up again and shuffled his feet; Elvis noticed this but did not react. We were all pleased with this session, as Elvis was very happy to spend time with us.

Max also went solo for his second round. He came in and did some send-offs to seated people. Again, this was completely new to him. Send-offs involve complete control on the part of the person, and Max has been spending much time exploring things at his own pace. Initially, he wanted to leave, but Patti sent him off to me, I clicked and treated him, asked him to sit, clicked and treated him for that, and sent him back to Patti. Patti then sent him off to Deb, who gave him a treat. He went toward the door and then back to Deb on his own. I suggested to Patti that she call him back, and when he came, to run out the door with him. Leaving the room was way more rewarding than any food treat at this time, and helped him to keep his stress level down by taking off some of the pressure.

When he came back in, Patti sent him to Marie, who successfully asked him to sit, twirl, and down. A few students noticed that Max flinches when he is being clicked by a stranger, so we stopped using the clicker at that time. Only Patti clicks for him now. Great observation! By now, he had a harder time focusing on visiting people. Patti sent him off to Kim, but he wouldn't go unless Patti actually moved with him, and then he stuck very close to her side. He managed a good send-off to Kristen and was very eager to leave the room. What a long session for Max, and two completely new activities for him!

Bailey also did a bunch of send-offs with everyone in the room. Kristen began by having Bailey come into the room and immediately go back out in a calming curve for focus. He then did a send-off to me, but he was not paying attention, so he left the room to regain focus. When he came back, he was able to do the send-off with me. I was seated but then stood up when he was in front of me, and he remained calm. He was slow in returning to Kristen, but managed to hold it together. Next, he went to Deb, who began in a seated position but stood up while he was in front of her. Each person did this with Bailey, and while the movement and change in body position was not a problem for him, he seemed to be a bit confused as to what was expected of him. We all find it amazing that he was able to do this tonight, as it wasn't long ago that we couldn't even look at him without him reacting strongly. Bravo for Bailey!

Shadow began his efforts to interact with the people in the room. He started out with good focus on Christi, but turned around and barked at Steve. He left the room, came back in and focused again on Christi. We started playing a game where each person, in turn, calls his name and tosses a few pieces of food at his front feet. I started, and he ate the treats. Kristen called his name, he turned around and looked at her, but she delayed tossing food for a second or two and he barked at her. We repeated this effort, and Kristen called and tossed food at the same time. Shadow didn't bark and did eat the food. She tried it a third time, and Shadow barked at her, so he left the room again. He had a difficult time calming himself down, even in the lobby, and when he came back into the room, he came to me and sat next to me for treats. This was definitely a very difficult situation for him.

So Christi sat down in a chair near the door and clicked and treated him for looking at her. After about a minute, Steve called Shadow's name. Shadow looked at Steve, took the treats that Steve tossed, returned his focus to Christi, then barked again. We decided that this was too much for him, so Christi got his focus, rewarded it, and took him out.

February Eighth

Present in 7:00 - 8:00 PM Class: Kristen and Bailey; Lisa and Indy; Deb and Elvis.

Tonight we broke into two groups of three and worked for an hour each. We did this because of concerns over very low temperatures. The plan was for each dog to have three minutes in each session. I also suggested to everyone that they spend a bit more time in the car with their dogs after a session, petting, praising and hanging out with them. Sometimes I worry that the dogs do a great thing and then just go back to the car and are left hanging, even after having a party. I want the dogs to go from aroused to calm with the owners as part of the deal. In addition, some dogs find being in the car a bit stressful, so having the person there for a bit longer can help. In the room I had placed a ring gate partially strung across the side area and left an agility tunnel roughly across the middle of the room to serve as a visual barrier for the smaller dogs.

We began our new adventure of using a round robin theme with Bailey and Elvis. Bailey came in the front door and did a few calming curves into the room. *See Illustrations 2-08a through 2-08d.* He started out with great focus. Kristen made her way to the side of the room, near the side door. The moment Deb brought Elvis through the front door, both Bailey and Elvis barked so they both left and regained their focus on their people. The second time they came in, Bailey barked again but Elvis managed to maintain his quiet focus on Deb. The third time Bailey came in he managed to stay quiet It was apparent that he was giving his all to Kristen, but Elvis had lost his attention on Deb so he went out. On the fourth attempt, both dogs were able to focus on their owners, but Kristen had taken Bailey out of sight. She did this to remove one distraction for him; he knew Elvis was there, but didn't see him. After about 30 seconds, Kristen brought Bailey in view, and Elvis barked. These two were having a rough time! The fifth time was a charm...both dogs came in and were able to

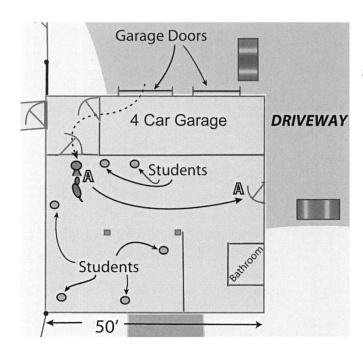

*Illustration 2-08a.
Dog A comes in
the front door and
focuses on his owner,
then makes his way
past people to the
side door.*

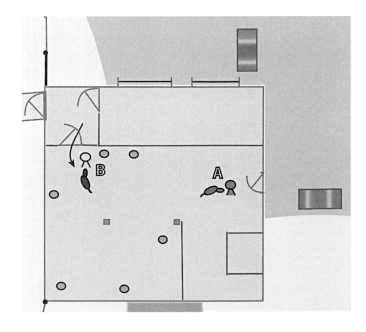

*Illustration 2-08b.
Dog B comes in
and focuses on her
owner, while Dog A
is with his owner on
the other side of the
room.*

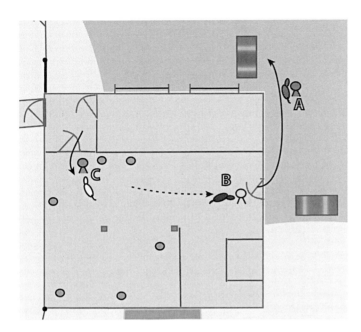

Illustration 2-08c. After a few minutes, Dog A leaves and takes a break in his car. Dog B makes her way toward the side door, then Dog C comes in the front door. Dog C and Dog B work together for a few minutes.

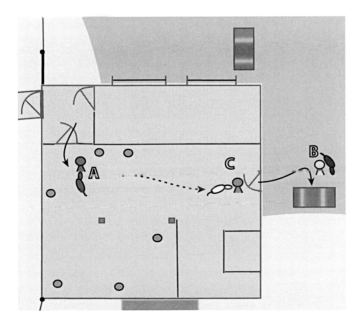

Illustration 2-08d. Dog B leaves and goes back to her car for a break, while Dog C makes his way to the side door. Dog A and Dog C work together for a few minutes, etc. For added variety, reverse the direction!

quietly pay attention to their people, responding to cues and getting rewards. We were all impressed that Bailey was able to bring himself back from the brink even after this much stimulation.

Bailey returned to his car and Elvis went to the side area while Lisa brought Indy in the front door. Indy's calming curves, her response to her name, is impressive. Elvis and Indy were both calm and able to handle this situation. Lisa sat down and worked Indy while Deb moved Elvis around a bit on the other side of the room. We had placed ring gates with a cloth across part of the side room area to give people the option of partially obscuring views of dogs. Elvis came into view and went out of it again, and Indy paid him no notice. We discussed the differences between Bailey, Indy and Elvis. Bailey is a very intense dog who always scans the room, but he is neutered. Elvis is intact, and we think there is no love lost between these two! Indy is also intact, but she is female. So we theorized that she would draw less negative reaction from the other dogs. Indy also scans the room less often then either Elvis or Bailey, so she probably comes off as being less confrontational than Bailey.

After three minutes, Elvis left the building (I love saying this!), Indy went to the side area, and Bailey came in the front door. Bailey was very eager to come in but was able to hold it together and focus. Indy was aware that there was another dog; she did a quick look, but returned her gaze immediately to Lisa. Kristen made her way to a chair; I suggested that if the humans are sitting, the dogs may take this cue to relax a bit. Indy's ears were focused for a while on Bailey while she worked for Lisa, but the entire three minute session was without reaction.

Indy went back to her car and Bailey made his way to the side of the room. Bailey became increasingly aroused, moving around more quickly and without purpose. But when Elvis came in the front door, they both were focused appropriately. Deb did her calming curve into the room and came back in, and again, both dogs were able to turn their backs on each other and ignore one another. They were even able to lie down facing their owners until Lisa walked into the room, and Elvis barked at her. Of course, Bailey responded to the barking, and this ended their session. Bailey returned to his car, and Elvis went to the side of the room.

As he did so, he was very interested in smelling where Bailey had been. Indy came in the front door. Again, these two were able to ignore each other in favor of getting rewards. Lisa did three calming curves into the room and made her way to a nearby chair. Several times, the dogs looked around and their eyes met (backs to each other, though) and both were able to immediately return their gazes to their owners!

At this time, it was suggested that we switch the direction of rotation so the dogs wouldn't become accustomed to a particular dog in a particular spot. These students are great! Lisa stayed in the front part of the room and Bailey came in the side door. He looked around for a long time but was still able to focus on Kristen. After three calming curves, they came in and Kristen sat. Initially, Bailey was managing to focus, but then began to lose it. Kristen tethered him to the wall because he was pulling. I wanted Kristen to not "play that game" with him. We never tether our dogs in reactive class, so this was a new experience for him. Bailey continued to focus on Elvis, and he was pulling hard enough for his front legs to come off the ground. Kristen waited for Bailey to turn to her so she could click him…he took the treat and went back to watching Elvis, huffing as he did so. Meanwhile, Elvis was doing a smashing job of completely ignoring Bailey! Wow! Bailey barked at him again, and Elvis continued to ignore him. At this point, their three minutes was up, so Deb went out with Elvis with a humongous party! Bailey was finally able to look at Kristen again, got clicked and treated and resumed his search for Elvis. He clearly was overstimulated. I suggested to Kristen that she walk away. He immediately looked for her as she walked away, so she was able to reward that. This was Bailey's third session, and it seemed that it was too much for him. The longer the sessions went, the more vigilant he was in his scanning and intent to bark.

For the last session of the first hour, Elvis came in the front door and immediately looked at Deb. Indy came in the side door and resumed her careful watch on Lisa. Both dogs really paid attention to their people, so Deb moved Elvis around a bit, doing some obedience moves and tricks. In order to challenge them a bit, since neither dog was giving any sign of stress at all, Deb sent Elvis through the tunnel, going away from Indy. Indy was curious but did not bark the first time. The second time Elvis went through the tunnel, though, she did bark, but turned right away from him. Elvis did not return the bark and Deb again took him out and had a great party!

Everyone really enjoyed this new version of class, and plan on doing this again next week.

Present in 8:00 - 9:00 PM Class: Patti and Max; Kim, Don and Mollie; Christi and Shadow.

Max was the first in the room, and needed 15 seconds of sniffing to look at Patti. Max still is not ready for a limitation on the amount of time he needs to focus, but the time he does take is diminishing nicely. Patti took Max to the side area and sat with him. Kim brought Mollie in the front door. Mollie also sniffed for ten seconds, at which point Kim took her out. I suggested to Kim that she not come so far into the room and to make sure to turn her shoulder to indicate to Mollie that she is continuing to move. While Mollie was sniffing, Max saw her and whined. The second time Mollie came in, she looked around, heard Patti's click for Max, went to the wall behind Kim, laid down curled up in a ball. Uh-oh. She was shutting down. Meanwhile, Max was whining again, to get to his friend. Kim, Don and I discussed Mollie's response, realizing quickly that the clicker possibly was the source of the issue, and asked Patti to put her clicker away. Mollie then noticed me, so in an effort to keep her subthreshold, I called her over to me (I was only a few feet away) to say hello and pet her. Whew. We brought Mollie back from the brink of shutting down. Her response to the room upon walking in the second time was very interesting. She looked around and couldn't believe all the people weren't there! This was something new to Mollie, and we know that anything new to Mollie is enough to shut her down completely. So I used myself as a **subsidence** measure against the "new" room. While this was going on, Max barked at us and Mollie replied with a bark, so they both left. When they returned, Mollie was still working but moving very slowly, and Max was not paying attention to Patti at all. Again he left, came back in, was able to do one hand target and left on a good note.

Mollie went to the side area and Shadow came in the front door. Christi forgot about the clicker, Mollie heard it and shut down. Christi put the clicker away – which is hard for all of us, including me, who are so conditioned to using it – and continued her calming curves into the room. Christi made her way to the nearby chair while Kim moved Mollie around a little bit on the other side of the room. Both dogs are doing very well, although Mollie is mostly out of view of Shadow. Near the end of their three minutes, I stood up and Shadow barked at me. Mollie did not respond to his bark, though! They both resumed working for their humans, and finished their session.

Shadow went to the side of the room and Patti brought Max in the front door. Max began his whining again, which resulted in Shadow barking. Both dogs left and returned several times and had trouble focusing. After a few entrances, both Patti and Christi sat in chairs. Max's focus on Shadow proved too much for Shadow, who had a very difficult time ignoring it. Max seemed unglued; he loves dogs so much that Patti was no match for their allure! In an attempt to redirect Max's attention from Shadow, I asked him to target and was able to click and treat him for this. I often dislike doing this because I am afraid that owners think I'm showing off, but this is not so. By asking Max to target, his attention left Shadow, who was now able to work. Max was able to target and take food from me while I was standing. This is improvement! He was more willing to work for me because I was a novelty, not because I'm better than Patti. Shadow left, and for a minute or two, we had Don (who was seated) toss treats from a short distance to Max. Max ended by being able to take food from Don's hand.

Max moved on to the side area and Mollie came in the front door. Don was now seated on the other side of the ring gates from Max and continued tossing food to Max. Since Max's big issue is fear of people, it seemed to me that we should continue in that vein while the alluring distraction of another dog was nearby. While it wasn't focus on Patti, it was better than getting nothing from him. Mollie worked fine for Kim, said hello to me, went back to working with Kim on sit at heel, bow, call front, and other skills. Max play-bowed to Don. This was clearly a conflict behavior because he stepped back as he bowed. I asked Don to only toss food to Max if his weight was not predominantly on his back legs, indicating more confidence. At the end of the three minutes, we allowed Max and Mollie to play. They were both offleash and played for about 1½ minutes. Mollie took this opportunity to approach several people for treats! Patti had trouble recalling Max (another big issue for him), so we agreed that the leash would remain attached next time. Once Kim had Mollie on her leash, Christi walked into the room. Mollie barked at her and Kim walked Mollie away, then approached Christi again. Mollie took food from Christi, and Max followed Mollie but did not take food. I was able to take Max gently by the collar, but he urinated when I did so. We are all sad when this happens.

Next, we switched the rotation order, as we did in the first hour. Mollie remained in the front and Shadow came in the side. He had to leave after ten seconds for lack of focus, but on his second entry, he looked at Christi in three seconds. Kim had Mollie's favorite treat, peanut butter. Shadow looked at Mollie and looked directly back at Christi without being called! Mollie was moving slowly and her eyes were very large. She was clearly worried or confused but managed to keep thinking. Shadow spent his entire session with a relaxed expression on his face, with one ear up and one ear down. Christi indicated that he does this when he's in "relaxed mode." The session ended without incident.

Shadow then walked toward the front of the room, right between me and Don, and didn't bat an eyelash! It didn't last long though; Max came in the side door and Shadow barked at him. He refocused quickly on Christi and continued to work well while Don worked with Max. He tossed treats at Max when Max's weight was evenly distributed between front and back, or if more of his weight was on his front legs. On the fourth treat, Max took it from Don's hand. This continued, but Max was unable to sit for a treat from Don.

Shadow went outside and Max came toward the front of the room. He paid little attention to Patti as he watched Mollie come into the room. Mollie worked well for Kim, eating all of her treats, but she still moved slowly, indicating her uncertainty with this new arrangement. Max took a treat from my hand after I walked up to him, then sat when I asked him to. This is a brave step for him, as standing people and people moving toward him usually makes him want to run. Don was also standing near him, but the moment Don's attention turned to Max, he backed away. Having a man stand near him and pay attention to him is still too difficult; we'll have Don remain sitting for a while with Max.

Finally, Mollie moved to the front of the room after Max left, and Shadow came in the side door. Shadow did an awesome job of coming into the room and immediately turning to watch Christi. It's great when dogs learn this routine and they try to turn around to their person even before they get through the door! Mollie remained calm and focused on Kim, but continued to move slowly. Patti came in the front door, and neither dog reacted! Patti crossed part of the room and sat down. Then Don crossed the room. Shadow looked over at him but did not bark, and returned his attention to Christi. Progress! Patti got up, walked across the room and back, and both dogs completely ignored her. This was a wonderful way to end the evening!

February Fifteenth

Tonight's weather was even more cold, windy and miserable than last week, so we again divided the class into two groups. Students were given the option of coming or staying home. Our format was similar to last week's class. I had the ring gates set up the same way as last week, but did not have the tunnel out.

We began our class with Mark's news of Yankee's exploits at the local dog park! He's gone three times so far, about once per week. Mark reported that Yankee will still bark at dogs while in the car, but once he's in the park and offleash, he no longer barks. He investigates smells, wanders around, wags his tail, does not cling too closely to Mark, and occasionally sniffs the butts of other dogs. He also allows other dogs to check him out. In the past, Yankee would react to other dogs by attempting to bite their butts. While Mark commented that Yankee is still anxious (drools), this is a tremendous improvement in Yankee's behavior! I warned Mark of two things: (1) Only attend the park occasionally, since stress is cumulative and this is still a stressful event for Yankee, and (2) be prepared in the event that Yankee suffers a setback of any kind, whether it's a sudden inability to tolerate the dog park or a general decline in his ability to tolerate other dogs. Variability of tolerance is part of the territory for a reactive dog, and having the expectation that this is a permanent change is likely to lead to heartache.

Elvis started us out by coming in the front door and doing send-offs to everyone. He is becoming more accustomed to this and thoroughly enjoying it! Yankee then came in the side door and did two calming curves with excellent focus. Deb played "Where's the puppy?" with Elvis, while Yankee did send-offs to me and then to Linda (who took notes for me tonight!). Yankee was so

eager to see everyone that he was hyper. Elvis' focus was exemplary, so I asked
Deb to walk a few steps toward Yankee and then do a call front. This resulted
in Elvis letting out a small "boof" toward Yankee, but he was able to continue
his work. Deb reported that his mouth was hard, so we ended the session.

Yankee moved to the side of the room while Mollie came in the front.
Mollie's responses were slow. Everyone needed repeated prompts to remember
to use their verbal markers, treat immediately and clearly ask for cues. I think
the 0° wind chills were getting to us all! On the third entry, Mollie's responses
became quicker and perkier. Yankee yelped at Mollie. This was not a reactive
noise, but an attempt to get her attention to play! Mollie continued to have a
hard time paying attention; she moved slowly but was better than last week.
Toward the end of the session, we had the dogs meet each other. The first
attempt resulted in Mollie lunging at Yankee. I reviewed the need to have the
dogs looking at the owners before sending them off to greet, the need to move
slowly, and to call the dogs away after three seconds. The dogs will follow the
owners if they turn their shoulders away from them. The second attempt was
less intense, but both dogs still had trouble. We did a third and final greeting,
and both dogs indicated that they wanted to meet but were conflicted about it.
They both were wagging, approach-avoiding, and acting quite sensitive about
the interaction. We ended the session quickly enough for it to be a success.

Mollie then went to the side area and Elvis came in the front with good
focus, but when he saw Mollie, he barked. Deb took him out of the room and
got his attention. Each time Deb brought Elvis back in, I noticed that she was
waiting until she came into the room and closed the door before she called him.
This allowed Elvis time to look around and find something to bark at. Deb also
has a bad habit (as do many of us) of yanking on the leash or dragging him
by the leash. We discussed this and I suggested that she call his name AS he
was walking through the doorway, and Elvis' focus immediately improved. He
began to come into the room and turn around to look at Deb so quickly that he
might as well have been moving backwards! He would also look at Mollie and
look back at Deb on his own, rather than waiting for her to call him. All this
time, Mollie did a stellar job of ignoring Elvis and his barking.

As Elvis went toward the side area, I reminded Deb that Elvis only has
ten seconds in which to respond to her cues, and that she needed to reward
him immediately when he did. We all tend to get lazy in this regard and forget
that this is a stressful time for our reactive dogs. Marie brought Yankee in and
walked toward Elvis. She called Yankee to her and Yankee ignored Elvis. Elvis
barked so Deb took him outside. Yankee then saw Mark and pulled toward
him; he seemed to be a bit anxious and was happy to see Mark. When Elvis
returned, he walked toward Yankee, straight on. Deb called him and he turned

to her immediately! We took turns greeting the dogs; Yankee did send-offs to Linda and Don, while Elvis greeted Mark. The significance of these greetings is that it adds distractions for the dogs, but it also gives them something else to focus on other than another dog. While Yankee is not reactive to people, Elvis can be, and his greeting of Mark was very appropriate.

Mollie came in the front door and Yankee moved to the side. The first time Mollie came in, she took four seconds to focus; the second time it was immediate. This is an improvement over recent sessions! Yankee worked on send-offs with Don while Mollie did the same with me. Mollie then did a send-off with Mark while he was standing. She did great, but didn't like his treat! While Mollie was doing send-offs with Mark, she looked over at Yankee, then back to Mark again. She woofed once at Yankee, but was able to continue working with Mark...astounding! Kim and Marie then sat in chairs approximately 12 feet away from each other and had their dogs lay down and focus on them. They did great, with no problems at all.

Mollie went to the side area and Elvis came in the front. Deb was quicker in her presentation of treats for this. Elvis saw Mark and took himself over to him without permission, so Deb called him back and then sent him over. Both dogs did several send-offs with various people with no issues. For variety, Deb then did some heeling with Elvis, and each dog looked at the other and chose to check in with his/her human. I reminded the humans to notice when the dog looks at another dog and chooses to check back in. This is definitely a time to reward!

Next it was Elvis' turn again to work with Yankee. Yankee saw Elvis and wanted to go to him; it looked like he wanted to play with Elvis, but he came right back to Marie when she called him. Both dogs consistently looked at each other and looked back at their people.

Yankee then had a turn to work with Mollie. When she came in, she focused immediately, but then started to look around the room. There were new people! Christi and Patti had arrived for their session, so Kim took Mollie to them to say hello to them and get treats. Both Christi and Patti were sitting in chairs. Yankee worked with Mark, and the dogs gradually got closer to each other as they worked. When they were about eight feet apart, Mark reported that Yankee's mouth was beginning to get hard, so each did one more send-off and we ended the session there.

Present in 8:00 - 9:00 PM Class: Christi and Shadow; Patti and Max.

Max started the session and had an incredibly difficult time coming into the room and looking at Patti. It was almost immediately clear that, like

Mollie, Max had become accustomed to a certain level of noise and activity that came with the larger group, and he also relied on the presence of another dog to be able to tolerate the stress of the situation. After several minutes with no focus, he heard some noises in another part of the building and completely shut down, so Patti took him back to the car.

Christi came in the side door with Shadow and slowly worked him toward the main area of the room. He did a send-off with me, did a small growl when he looked around the room, but returned to Christi. Because we want to work on his ability to tolerate people looking at him, I tried the activity we ended with last week where I called his name and when he looked at me I tossed treats at him. He was fine with this, and I did it several times, but then he started to bark at me. It was a demand bark for more treats! This sudden change in activity seemed to unravel him. He was unable to check back in with Christi so he went back to his car.

Max's turn again. He saw Christi come in the side door and whined a bit, looking for Shadow. After only a short time, he looked at Patti, who was instructed to be incredibly excited that he looked at her. This was so difficult for Max; he was so worried and skittish that he didn't take treats. It's difficult to work with a dog who won't eat. The quiet in the room was unsettling for him, and he began to pull toward the door. He tried this several times. We ended the session when Max finally looked at Patti and she clicked and the reward was that he got to leave.

Shadow came in again and displayed wonderful attention, and although he barked once at the others in the room he returned his gaze to Christi immediately. She walked him through the room again, and in between people who were sitting only about five feet apart! Christi's tendency is to ask for behaviors more than once, and when walking, to wait too long to reward, so we worked on these things. Shadow needed to have a high rate of reinforcement for the leash walking through a group of people because it was a high-stress situation. She clicked and treated him almost every two to three steps. He didn't bark once during this exercise!

We then brought Max in the front door while Shadow was at the side. Max saw Shadow and immediately whined; he wanted to play. Shadow growled at him, but this didn't deter Max. Shadow was able to turn back to Christi for a short period of time, but then barked at Max again. Max continued to look at Shadow and whine, but was able to turn back to Patti briefly. Shadow found Max's staring to be difficult, and he alternated between lunging/growling/barking at Max and turning back to Christi. Each time he looked back and Christi, she clicked and treated, but after the first few times, I suggested she not call him back. She tried this, and after only three more repetitions, he returned his focus to Christi more quickly.

Shadow went out for a break. Christi felt that he was doing really well and wanted to take some pressure off of him. When he came back in, Max was staring at him again. This time, though, Shadow gave no reaction to this! Yay for Shadow! Christi had Shadow walk a few steps in different directions, closer and then farther away from Max.

Max, meanwhile, began to take treats from me and from Linda. Since this is such a difficult situation for Max, and because we really want to help him to like interactions with people, I felt that we needed to get what benefit we could from this session. Since he was paying little attention to Patti and focusing mainly on Shadow, we used Shadow's **subsidence** effect to our benefit. Max started wagging while taking treats from me and Linda, and when Linda stopped to write these notes, he barked at her for more treats! Holy cow!

I explained to Christi the "Look at that" game, and she started clicking Shadow each time he looked at Max. He was okay four times, but then he barked at Max. Christi then added the cue, "Where's the dog?" when he looked at Max and just before she clicked. Shadow continued to bark at Max each time he looked at him. Christi asked him to sit, and he did. She repeated this several times, and he continued to bark. Just when we thought he was past thinking, he play bowed to Max!

All right, so now we had a new situation here. Patti and Christi slowly walked toward each other, sent their dogs off to sniff each other for a count of three and then called their dogs away from each other. See *Photos 2-15a through 2-15e.* We reviewed the rules before they actually proceeded. They did a great job of not pulling on the dogs' leashes, getting focus before sending them off and remaining calm at the count of three. The activity was repeated and both dogs remained interested and calm. The third time, the dogs progressed to butt sniffing and play bows. Shadow had a high waggly tail. Both dogs had relaxed faces. They licked noses, and I had Christi drop Shadow's leash. We did this because I knew that Max loves dogs and would be unlikely to be worried about being trapped by a leash. But we didn't know what Shadow would do, so we wanted him to feel uninhibited by a leash. It seemed appropriate to have one of the two attached to a leash for management. It went well. Shadow went to Linda for a treat – another first! Shadow seemed to be more interested in food than Max. They did play a bit, though, and Max tried to hump Shadow. Shadow's correction was very appropriate, but we called them away from each other to be safe. We had them have one last sniff to end on a good note, and ended our session. If I remember correctly, Christi's words were, "I think I'm going to cry!"

Photos 2-15a through 2-15e. In this sequence, taken a few weeks after this class, you can see: (a) Shadow is interested in seeing Mollie (to the right of the camera). (b) He is anxious about seeing her, as evidenced by the stress lick. (c) Christi gets Shadow's focus (Kim is getting Mollie's, too).

(d) Both owners tell their dogs to "go see" and walk slowly toward the other dog. (e) The dogs sniff noses; their body postures relax. (f) The owners call their dogs back to them after only three seconds. Success!

February Twenty-Second

Present: Deb and Elvis; Kristen and Bailey; Lisa and Indy; Kim, Don and Mollie; Marie and Yankee; Christie and Shadow; Patti and Max.

This session centered mainly on each dog working with Acacia. For the past several weeks, we have been really pushing these dogs to their limits; tonight we removed some of that pressure so the dogs could really be successful. I began by having Acacia at the back of the room, as far away from the door as possible, with her laying down and facing me so she would be as unobtrusive as possible. Each dog's session lasted approximately 3½ minutes.

Elvis began the session – he worked without Acacia in the room. He came in the room and had great focus right off the bat, but quickly became distracted by Don and wanted treats from him, so Deb took him out of the room. When she brought him back in, he was moving more slowly but was responding to her cues. Christi came in the side door and Elvis barked at her, so Deb took him out again. He repeated his exit and entry several more times due to lack of focus. I asked Deb to be more proactive in asking him to do things, giving him a job. As soon as she started to do this, he remained on task without incident. She was then able to send him to different people for send-offs and treats. Elvis finished his session in a happy, eager manner.

I brought Acacia in and we situated ourselves at the back of the room. Kristen had a hard time even getting Bailey's attention outside the front door; we could hear his whining for several minutes. When he did come in, he was able to look at Kristen with no trouble. Then he saw Acacia and gave her a long look. Kristen took him out. When she brought him back in, I gave her the same suggestion I had given Deb; that our dogs do much better when we give them jobs. As soon as she began to be more directive with Bailey, his focus increased. He looked at Acacia and then back at Kristen. Then he looked at Acacia again, and pulled on his leash to get to her, but turned back to Kristen.

Yay! He continued to look at her and back to Kristen until his time was up. Kristen needs to make sure she's getting a treat to Bailey more quickly after she clicks. I shared some information with the class on a study which had been done by Jesus Rosales-Ruis and his graduate students at the University of Northern Texas. In this study, he delayed reinforcement delivery by five seconds after the click. Even dogs who were very clicker savvy had trouble with this delay; they became anxious and exhibited superstitious behaviors.

Indy was next. Her focus on Lisa was very intent. She wandered to Don, who was sitting nearby, but went right back to Lisa. She then wandered over to Linda, and then went back to Lisa. Of course, Lisa clicked and treated all of Indy's attention on her. Indy then looked right at Acacia and back at Lisa. Over the course of Indy's session, I increased Acacia's motion level, from down, to sit, to stand, to moving around and doing spins, etc. Indy was able to go visit people and return to Lisa while tolerating Acacia's movements.

Yankee came into the room all wound up! He was very eager to see people but contained himself enough to return to Marie when she called him. I ran Acacia through increasing levels of motion again, and Yankee managed to do what was asked of him with no reaction to Acacia. I even heeled Acacia around the room, and Yankee tolerated this easily.

When Mollie came in, she gave a calming lick, held her head down, appeared to be very subdued, but gave good focus to Kim. She was interested in visiting with the people in the room but maintained her good response level to Kim. Once Kim was satisfied that Mollie was paying attention, she began to send Mollie off to greet people. Mollie immediately perked up and became excited. Again, I took Acacia through her paces, starting with a calm down and moving up in posture and motion level. By the end of Mollie's session, Acacia was doing jump-up hand targets and Mollie gave her no notice at all. Wow!

I put Acacia away and Christi brought Shadow in the side door. He maintained good focus on Christi and ignored the humans in the room. Christi walked him around the room, behind where people were sitting, so he could take treats from peoples' hands held behind their backs. We do this so he doesn't have to look at scary faces while accepting treats from strangers. First he came to me and took treats from me while I said hello to him. Then he took a treat from Kristen's outstretched hand, and did the same from Marie's hand. He repeated this for Deb and Patti. But then Deb moved and Shadow barked at her. Christi instinctively pulled Shadow away so we talked about that. Christi got Shadow's focus and then took him out of the room to end the session.

Max came in the side door and only gave Patti a brief look after 25 seconds. He did not take the treat she offered. I quickly told Patti to enthusiastically move toward the people the next time he looked at her because he seemed to want to go see the people. It took him 20 seconds to look at her again, so she moved about half the distance to the closest person. He needed another 25 seconds to look at Patti again, and then got to Deb to take a treat out of her hand. He moved around behind where people were sitting, and took treats from their hands held behind them. He took a treat from me, Kristen, Marie and Christi, and then sat for Patti. His reward for that was to leave the room. Great job for Max!

For the second round, Indy came in the side door and Elvis came in the front. Both dogs began the session with great focus on their owners. Indy went to Kim to say hello and Elvis lunged at Indy. Indy barked at Elvis and Elvis barked in response to her bark, so both dogs went out. I realized that I set them up to fail because the send-offs I arranged necessitated the dogs facing each other. Oops! Instructor error! When they returned, they again began with great focus. Elvis went to Marie and Indy went to Patti, and they were set up so they moved perpendicular to each other, not head on. Elvis looked twice at Indy but stayed on target. Each dog continued to visit with people without paying attention to each other until the session ended.

Mollie and Yankee began their session also with great focus, and ignored each other. Yankee went to Linda to say hello and Mollie went to Patti. Both dogs were fine with the movement of the other, but Mollie became unsure of herself halfway to Patti. Kim called her back and started over, and Mollie was much better the second time, with only a very slight hesitation and a waggly tail. Mollie then went to Christi and was very enthusiastic in her greeting. Yankee and Mollie then slowly approached each other to say hello. Yankee let out a "yip" of excitement, to which Mollie responded with a lifted lip. Marie and Kim called their dogs away, got their focus and sent them off to greet each other a second time. Yankee lunged at Mollie; this is too exciting for him, so we ended their session with focus on their owners.

I brought Acacia back in for Bailey's session and settled at the back of the room again. Bailey was pawing at the door to get in, so Kristen again had to wait for him to be calm enough to enter. He was all over the place when he did come in, scanning, pulling and staring. Acacia, a bit concerned, turned around to look, and Bailey barked, so he left. On his third attempt to come in, he finally sat. Kristen's goal was to reward any calm behavior. He looked over at Acacia when her tags jingled, but turned back to Kristen. He did the same thing when Don made a rustling noise. Every little sound was a giant cause for concern for Bailey, so stimulated was he. Kristen continued to click Bailey for any of his calmer behaviors, and I was able to have Acacia sit, then stand, then sit again, and Bailey was able to tolerate it. He eventually laid down, but continued to give Acacia intense looks any time she moved. He ended the session by taking treats from Kristen with a very hard mouth, so we know that this was an extremely difficult challenge for him.

Shadow had a better time of it. He had good focus on Christi and ignored Acacia. He went to Patti for treats, and didn't even need to be behind her to do it!

Photo 2-22a. Shadow has begun to learn that people mean good things. His "relaxed ear," balanced stance, and open mouth smile all indicate that he is calm.

But he wouldn't return to Christi – he liked Patti's treats – so Patti turned her back on him and Shadow returned to Christi. He then went back to Patti for more treats and then to Kristen for whom he sat for treats. Again, he was facing Kristen. Big improvement! At this time, he looked over at Acacia and was able to look away from her and back at Christi. Wonderful!

Max came into a dogless room and immediately whined with excitement. He turned to Patti when she called him but turned his head right back to the group. When he did look at her again, she took him toward Kim, where he crept and stretched to get a treat. He did take food from Christi, but wilted when he realized that everyone was looking at him. We began to take turns calling his name and tossing him a treat, like we used to do. He worked the crowd, and even took a treat from Lisa, who was new to him. Max became so bold as to whack at Christi's leg for a treat! He sat for Patti and ended his session.

Indy came in the side door and Elvis came in the front. Both dogs were extremely focused on their owners and ignored each other, even as they practiced their send-offs with people. Elvis was even checking in with Deb without being called! Yay for Elvis! He did lots of double-takes toward Indy but didn't bark or lunge at all. Deb did some "Where's the puppy?" with Elvis, and he did fine. Indy finished her session by giving Kristen a kiss!

We increased Bailey's time back up to ten seconds, since he's been having such a difficult time maintaining focus. The third time he came into the room, he checked in with Kristen within four seconds. But he continued to scan and whine with excitement. We did not use Acacia for this session with him because Kristen wanted to practice having Bailey greet people. He first went to Marie, and he was very attentive to her. He sat, targeted and shook a paw for Marie, then returned quickly to Kristen. Kristen then sent him off to Christi. He watched Kim's movement but did not bark at her. Great improvement.

Yankee and Mollie repeated their session from earlier. Mollie came in the side door and focused nicely. Yankee came in the front and was very hyper, wandering around and only returning to Marie when she called him. Mollie was moving slowly and we realized that Marie was using a clicker, so we asked her to put it away. Mollie visibly relaxed after that. Yankee worked with Don on greetings while Mollie visited with Patti. Both dogs were sitting, and Yankee was calming down. Marie sent Yankee to Christi while Mollie went to Don. At this point the dogs were a mere eight feet away from each other, back to back. Yankee looked at Mollie. They continued to do their greetings, working around each other in a circle with their backs to each other. Mollie started to have a hard mouth, so Kim finished her session.

Shadow came into the room when Max was already inside. Max had no focus at all because he wanted to play with Shadow. Max's focus on Shadow made Shadow very uncomfortable, and Shadow also was being handled by Pat. Shadow started out with great focus on Pat, but Pat is not as accustomed to the protocols as Christi, so I was helping him by telling him what to do and when to reward. But Max is afraid of men, so this session was even harder for Max. Shadow did a few things for Marie for treats. Patti took Max to the side of the room, but still he was unable to focus. This session, unfortunately, ended without great success. There were too many challenges for Max, and Shadow was being handled by someone who didn't have as much practice in class, so he was having a hard time, too. Next week we will make sure that we minimize the distraction level for these dogs so they can be successful.

Where Are They Now?

While the journeys of the players in this book are not yet over, you may want to know where they are and what they are doing. The best I can do is to tell you what they were doing at the time this book went to press.

Mollie

Mollie continues to attend class. She recently decided that it was okay to play with both Max and Bing at the same time, but had no trouble telling Max off when he was a bit rambunctious! During class, she routinely approaches people to say hello and get a treat for sitting, even if the person is a complete stranger. Her walks in the park are pretty much that...a walk in the park. She can walk by groups of people and dogs and not make a sound. Occasionally, she has a difficult time in a tight situation, but clearly is learning to tolerate new sights and sounds.

Bailey

Bailey is in the process of moving to new digs where he will have a fence! The effects of the stress of moving remain to be seen, but Linda has embarked on a renewed effort to focus on loose leash walking. He continues to have a more difficult time with dogs than he does with people, and Kristen is more committed to enforcing her expectations for focus. Recently, Bailey approached several complete strangers in the class, and his demeanor was calm and friendly. He also recently met a new dog who belongs to a friend of Kristen's. Bailey's behavior indicated that he was very conflicted as to what to do with the dog. He sniffed at and barked at the other dog, and seemed to want to interact but didn't quite know how to proceed. Given his behavior toward other dogs while on leash, this is not surprising. I hope to have him practice sniffing Acacia's tail in an effort to teach him what to do, but this requires that he be calm in her presence. We still have much work to do.

Maggie

Colleen and Tracy bought a pup a few weeks after Maggie started to attend class. The pup became ill and required much time and attention. Given Maggie's improvement in her ability to focus on Colleen, and her learned enjoyment of hand targeting, they decided to finish the weeks they paid for and work on their own. They continue to manage Maggie and are having continued success with her.

Spencer

Laura's work schedule changed and she was unable to continue to bring Spencer to class. Laura bought a house and is able to provide better management and a calmer household for Spencer than he previously had. While he remains highly reactive, Laura reports that her confidence level in handling him has increased greatly.

Elvis

Deb made the very difficult decision to have Elvis neutered. Upon his return to class, his movement appeared to be a bit slower and more relaxed. He was able to work quietly and calmly throughout the entire class, even when working along with dogs to whom he typically reacts highly. Deb reports that Elvis is still reactive to the neighbor dogs on either side of his fence, but she is working out a training program to address this. Deb still hopes to return to agility with him some day.

Yankee

Yankee is learning to look calmly at other dogs without reacting. For many months, Yankee staunchly refused to look at other dogs at all in class. It seemed that he had learned his job too well! But this is not the goal for him, so Marie and Mark have spent time working on rewarding calmly looking toward other dogs. Marie has also spent time keeping Yankee's attention on her when he comes to class; he gets very excited to see all the people and stops paying attention to her. Some of this is avoidance; if he interacts with people, he doesn't have to look at the dogs. But he had become rather pushy with his interactions, so Marie has made her expectations much clearer of late.

Max

Max continues to attend class. Last week, Patti walked him past Marie at a distance of about 20 feet and with each pass, Marie tossed a handful of hot dog pieces at him. They slowly closed their distance, and with little to no effort, Max decided that he liked Marie enough to march right up to her with a waggly tail and take treats out of her hand! If we didn't know that Max would be terrified if we all jumped up and celebrated, we would have! He was selective over who he is comfortable with at this time, but his demeanor during this exercise was so incredibly heartening! We all hope that he can generalize this to many other people in different environments. Patti reports that while she sometimes still has to carry him on parts of their walk, he is now taking treats at times during their walks; this is a definite improvement.

Shadow

As quickly as Shadow entered class, he progressed through it and graduated himself! Shadow came to class for three months. In that time, he went from being reactive to people anywhere within 50 feet to having no trouble walking by people within a few feet. By the time he left the group, he was happily visiting with each human student regardless of whether they were standing or sitting. This behavior generalized to outside locations, not just here at class but also at home on walks. Yay for Shadow!

Indy

Lisa had trouble continuing with the class due to her new job. Indy's behavior at class was quite impeccable, but this was not immediately translating to other environments. Lisa decided to spend time at dog shows working Indy on reactive behavior activities at a distance from the action. Over time, and in just a few shows, Indy's behavior improved greatly to the point where she was not reacting at all. Lisa made the decision to send Indy to her breeder so the breeder could show her in conformation. The breeder reports that Indy has no trouble getting along with any human or canine. The only reasoning we can use is that Indy learned a habit of reacting in the presence of Lisa. Without Lisa around, Indy's behavior is different. It will be interesting to see what happens on Indy's return.

Acacia

Acacia continues to love doing her reactive dog work, teaching other dogs about what they should do (of course she also loves to work for treats!). Her reactivity on walks continues to be subsided by the presence of Bing, who loves to greet and play with other dogs. Bing gets to the dogs first, and when Acacia approaches, she is much calmer.

Never the End

The dedication of the humans at the other ends of these leashes bears mention. Having a reactive dog is not what anyone imagines when they go to pick out their pup or rescue their next companion. For some folks, the prospect of this work is simply too much to bear. They return the dog or keep the dog at home, away from the things which make him bark. Some people become fascinated with the process of learning and of developing a working relationship, so they come to class and just keep coming. Others are motivated by the progress they see and are eager to see more. Often, they 'just want to be able to walk the dog'. And occasionally, I see someone who has a loftier goal, such as being able to do agility again.

It is up to the owners to decide when they are ready to leave the class. The dog will always be reactive. The class is there as a means for supporting the human who is supporting the fearful dog. Students can join the class for as long as they like. If they leave and feel that at some time later they need to return, they are welcome. The stimuli to which a dog may be reactive can change over time. My goal is to enable owners to think for themselves, to look at the stimuli and the rewards and develop their own programs for working with their dogs. None of us have all the answers, and the group allows us to put our heads together. After a student leaves, he or she is welcome to remain on the Yahoo! group so they may stay in touch and ask questions. Many friendships of the human variety have developed through this group, and that's an added bonus.

I was tempted to continue writing up the notes from each week's class. Every session has new developments, new activities. But I knew that if I did that, the length of the book would be ridiculous! The point at which I stopped writing notes was purely random. The dog and student teams continue to come to class, learn new things, have ups and downs and build their working relationships. We continue to provide the best we can for our dogs, and we will continue to love our dogs despite their shortcomings. And we continue to know that our dogs trust us and love us.

Flying Solo...

When You Don't Have A Reactive Dog Class Nearby

While the emphasis of this book is on the structure of a reactive dog class as run by a positive trainer, the material herein also pertains to those of us who have a reactive dog but live far from a positive trainer who runs a reactive dog class. Let's take a look at how we can accomplish some great training successes with a reactive dog in this situation.

Using the chapter called, "In the Physical Realm" as a guide, you can use real life situations as your reactive dog class.

1. **A Large Space:** In our reactive dog classes, we utilize a large space so that we may keep the dogs' arousal levels below threshold level. Before working your dog on your own, you must know what your dog's triggers are and what your dog's arousal threshold level is for each trigger.

   For example, Acacia is reactive to dogs. She is almost nonreactive at dog shows and when we walk in busy public areas, but has trouble when seeing dogs in more rural or quiet settings. She has the most trouble with boisterous dogs, young dogs (she is terrified of puppies!) and dogs moving toward her. Offleash dogs running toward her is a guaranteed melt-down. Her threshold level is one foot of distance at a dog show, ten feet in busy public areas, 20 feet with boisterous, young dogs or puppies, and 50 feet with dogs moving toward her. Offleash dogs running toward her stimulate her above her threshold level for arousal the moment they appear on the radar screen. In all cases, her younger brother, Bing, has a subsidence effect on her threshold level.

   I must have more space available to me than my dog's threshold level in order to be successful at working my dog on her reactivity. For many dogs, this means finding huge spaces. Parking lots and park-like settings are often ideal for these situations. Parks with multiple playing fields can be very useful when you need lots of space.

2. **Ample Parking for Cars:** This requirement is actually related to #1 above in the sense that you must be able to park your car far enough away from the stimuli you are working on so that your dog does not react when he is in the car. Your dog needs to be able to be calm and quiet in his car in between work sessions; the car is a place of safety, solace, comfort, and reflection. When you get your dog out of the car, you and he will be moving closer to the stimuli rather than the other way around.

3. **Minimum of Distractions:** The fewer distractions you have during a session, the more control you will have over the effect of one stimulus. Let's say that I want to work with Acacia on her reactivity toward joggers. I know that I can go to Cedar Creek Park on a weekday morning after rush hour and find a mostly empty park. It has two parking lots and a 1¼ mile track. If I want to stay near the car so that I have the maximum amount of control over her and the environment, I can just hang out with her in the parking lot and wait for joggers to go past us. I can see them coming, I can manipulate the environment so that she can either see the jogger coming from a distance (by standing with her away from the car) or see him with very little warning by using my car as a visual barrier for her (by standing very close to the car), and I can put her back in the car if she is unable to see the jogger and check in with me. I can also chose to select which stimuli I want to address by moving her out of view of cyclists and people with strollers, if I don't want to work on those stimuli at that time.

   Over time, I can choose to go to that park at more busy times, say, at 7:00 am or 5:00 pm, when most folks are not at work. The park is usually busier and will allow for more opportunities to practice Acacia's new behavior of, "see the jogger, look at Mommy and get clicked and treated."

4. **Barriers -- Natural and Otherwise:** In the above example, I used my car as a visual barrier. Depending on where you choose to work, you may be able to use a hedge, a wall, a tree, a fence, or just about any solid object as a way to prevent your dog from seeing certain stimuli. Of course, you want your dog to see the stimuli you are addressing, but you may wish to block his visual access to certain other stimuli, or from a stimulus which may be too intense for your dog at that time.

   You can also use your house as a barrier! Most reactive dog owners have trouble getting out the front door with their dogs because they live in a suburban or urban location, which means an almost constant stream of stimuli from the time the door opens (and sometimes sooner). One of the toughest activities you can do with your reactive dog is to open the front door, take one step outside with your dog, and have him look up at you within a reasonable period of time and without reacting to a potpourri of stimuli. If you treat your front door as if it's your car, you can put your dog back inside the house if he reacts or if he is unable to focus on you. This is truly an important task to undertake, and its value can't be overstated. If you wish to walk your dog around the neighborhood, this first step (literally and figuratively) is absolutely critical.

5. **Variety of People, Dogs and Distractions:** For the most part, this category can be addressed by selecting a venue at different times. If your dog is reactive to people, you may wish to spend some time parking your car at the periphery of a large parking lot associated with a shopping center or mall. There will be times, for certain, when few people will be walking about. Other times, the place will be a madhouse. Typically, the busier it is, the more variety of people you will encounter, and along with it, the more distractions you will see. Dogs do not generalize well at all, so take into consideration the need to park in different areas of a particular parking lot, at different times of the day, and facing different directions. You will also need to visit more than just one place; if you regularly visit the Crest Plaza, you should also visit another shopping center on different occasions. If you don't take care to do this, your dog will likely only learn his new skills at the Crest Plaza, and his skills will not generalize to Village West shopping center.

Take into account the need to only work one variable at a time. If your dog is reactive to children, then start driving to playing fields. Park as peripherally as possible. Perhaps you can work on your dog's focus just outside your car when T-ball practice is just beginning. The kids are all arriving and going away from you, toward the field. There is little threat there, from the dog's perspective, because the children are generally facing away from him and going away from him. As soon as they convene for practice, end your session and leave the area. Over subsequent training sessions, you can park a bit closer (maybe ten feet each time), to diminish the distance threshold of arousal. As your dog is better able to handle this situation calmly, you may want to work on the "kids running and screaming" aspect of reactivity. Arrive at the park a bit later, so that the kids have already arrived and are starting to practice, but park your car as far away as possible again. You are increasing the difficulty level for your dog (increasing the motion aspect), so decrease the intensity of as many of the other stimuli as possible (distance, in this example). Another variable might be the number of kids present; begin to work with your dog at a practice where there aren't many kids. Later on, after your dog has achieved the ability to focus on you calmly when there are a dozen kids running and making noise at a distance of 100 feet, you may want to work your dog when there is a game or a tournament, or multiple games or practices going on. This way, you may increase the number of children present. Another variable to consider may be the ages of the kids. Look at as many variables as you can that correspond to the reactive stimulus.

6. **Small Class:** This category corresponds to the number of distractions or stimuli present at any one time. When you are working on your own, you must think from a dog's perspective. If my dog is dog-reactive, and I work her in a quiet park on a day when we may only see one or two dogs in a training session, I must be aware of the fact that she can see the dog, smell the dog, hear the dog's tags, smell the scent of the dozens of dogs who visited yesterday, hear the dog across the street from the park who is barking at her and racing up and down the edge of her property along the electric fence line, see the joggers on the other side of the park (to which she is also reactive), and smell the dropped pieces of bread and hot dog left on the ground yesterday by some children. All of these things are distractions which are difficult to control! The fewer of these distractions that exist, the better response I will likely get.

    You can accomplish quite a lot with your reactive dog without the benefit of a group class once you understand the basic element of behavior science. Classes offer support for the humans, but there are online groups for dog training which can provide that support. Exercises can sometimes be difficult to implement when you're alone, but they are rarely impossible. Even calming curves with a dog can be done with an unknowing partner! Once you have spent time successfully getting and keeping your dog's attention when another dog is at, say, 50 feet, take three steps toward the other dog, then pivot and walk away, clicking and treating as your dog's head disengages from viewing the other dog. It will be a bit more challenging to do this way because you are less likely to know what the other dog will do.

The way to improve your chances of success is probably to start from a farther distance than you might if you were in a class.

Finally: keep a log of what you work on, where, how long, your success rate, time of day, etc. Document as many variables as possible about each session so you can compare it to other sessions. Give your dog sufficient downtime between mini sessions and at least two days between training days. Try to meet up with other people who have similar dogs and similar training philosophies. This, of course, can be easier said than done, but not impossible. Most of all, think in terms of tiny successes!

Glossary of Terms and Concepts

Call Fronts: An obedience skill. You start with your dog on your left side (heel position) and take several steps backward while calling your dog. Your dog turns and comes toward you and sits directly in front of you, with his toes nearly touching your toes.

Calm in the Car: A dog who remains quiet (no barking or whining) and finds a comfortable position (sitting or laying down) in which to remain for extended periods of time. The dog should be in a covered crate or in a seatbelt with the windows covered so that he can't see out and look for things at which to bark.

Calming Curves: An exercise where two dog/handler teams begin at some predetermined distance (often 100 feet) from each other, walk toward each other, and turn away from each other, returning at the starting point. The dogs are rewarded at the moment they disengage their focus on the approaching dog. More reactive dogs need to start from a larger distance. At first, each team only takes three steps toward each other; they progress to 15 or 20 steps, depending on the starting distance.

Calming Signals: A term coined by Turid Rugaas, a Norwegian dog trainer. This has become a rather mainstream term in dog training circles. It refers to any number of body language signals which dogs display toward other dogs, people or other species which indicate one of three things: (1) I don't intend to harm you; (2) you are excited and I am trying to calm you down; or (3) I am excited and I need to calm myself down. Examples of calming signals include nose licking, avoiding eye contact, looking away, turning away, moving very slowly, play bowing, yawning, or stretching. If a dog is not sure what to do, he may engage in calming signals, also sometimes known as **displacement behaviors**.

Checking In: The dog looks at (checks in with) his owner. The result is that he gets clicked and treated.

Classical Conditioning: The behavioral technique made famous by Ivan Pavlov in his study of salivary glands in dogs. It is also known as "associative learning" or "Pavlovian learning," and involves the association of one stimulus with another. There is no conscious thought process taking place during classical conditioning, so many repetitions often need to be done in order to strengthen the association between the two things. A simple example is the Stuff-a-Dog activity: place a treat in the dogs' mouth and then say his name. With enough repetitions, the dog will begin to look toward the human who is saying his name; it comes as a knee-jerk response.

Clicker: A marker which is usually a piece of metal crimped onto a piece of plastic, often with a tab for easy attachment to a keychain. The purpose of the clicker is to teach the dog the association between the clicker sound and a treat (short term), and to teach the dog that the click indicates that he's done something that the person likes and he will be rewarded for it (long term). The clicker marks the behavior you are looking for. Imagine using it like a camera; you're taking a picture of a behavior you like. Often, the clicker is used as a signal to end the behavior the dog is emitting.

Clomicalm® (Novartis): A selective serotonin (5-HT) reuptake inhibitor used as an aid in the treatment of separation-related disorders manifested by destruction and inappropriate elimination (defecation and urination) in combination with behavioral modification techniques.

Counterconditioning: A classical conditioning process in which the underlying emotional response to a stimulus is changed, usually from negative to positive. We almost always do this by pairing food with the stimulus from a distance far enough away that the dog doesn't react. Over time and many repetitions, the distance is decreased so that the dog can handle being close to the once-scary stimulus.

Displacement Behavior (see Calming Signals)

Finish Lefts: The second part of the call front sequence. From the call front, where the dog is sitting in front of the handler, the dog is cued to move toward the rear of the person on the left side, turn in toward the person, and sit. The dog ends up sitting on the left side of the person (heel position), facing the same direction as the handler.

Flooding: This is the process of bombarding a dog with a stimulus of which he's afraid (without causing physical harm) until his fearful response ceases. Flooding, at one time, was thought to be a very effective tool. We now believe that not only is it inhumane due to the high levels of stress it causes; it is often also not as effective as other techniques, such as counterconditioning and systematic desensitization.

Fun Recalls: A favorite activity for many dogs! This involves having a handful of treats and a dog in front of you. Your feet should be shoulder width apart. Begin by showing the dog a treat, then placing it between your feet. Click as the dog eats the treat. When the dog backs up, show him another treat and place it between your heels. Click when he eats the treat. When the dog backs up again, place another treat on the ground behind your heels, and click when the dog eats the treat. It is important to be showing him where the treat is going or he'll lose his focus on it. As you start tossing treats far enough behind you, the dog will go through your legs. When he does this, stand up and turn around, and you'll have your dog in front of you again! Now you can start calling him and tossing a treat through your legs, clicking as he commits to going between your legs. The farther you can toss the treats, the more time you'll have to stand up and turn around.

Generalize: The process of learning the same skill in different environments. An environment can include different people, animals, smells, proximities, levels of activity, level and type of noise, and amounts of these things. Since dogs do not generalize well, we need to help them to be successful in many different environments before we can expect our dogs to be able to respond to our cues consistently. This is one of the biggest tripping points of most dog owners; most humans figure that once the dog learns a skill in the kitchen, he can do it everywhere else. Not true!

Hard/Soft Mouth: Describes how rough or gently the dog takes a treat from your hand. A hard mouth is almost always associated with an increased level of arousal. We usually will move the dog away from the stimulus or situation when we notice a hard mouth.

Having a Party: This is the celebration at the end of a great working session. It should last at least 20 seconds, takes place in the car or the dog's crate, and involves the use of as many reinforcers as possible. This also gives the dog a break from the challenging task of focusing on the owner. And, it helps to differentiate between a job well done and a job poorly done with lack of focus. We often joke to each other that we want to "hear the party!"

Kong®: A hollow rubber toy which can be stuffed with all kinds of yummy treats which your dog can then unstuff. It comes in a variety of colors and sizes and can be frozen for longer chewing satisfaction. A Kong can keep your dog busy during downtime; the licking and chewing action can actually help your dog relax.

Live Bait: A loving term jokingly referring to a person who functions as a distraction in our training endeavors. Live bait can be a person who just happens to be near to where you are training, or it can be someone you ask to help you. Usually live bait involves little to no interaction with the dog, but sometimes it can involve tossing food at the dog or doing a send-off. As with any distraction, the live bait often starts quite a distance from the dog, and over time, becomes closer to the dog or moving more quickly near the dog.

Longline: A leash which is longer than six feet. It has a clip on one end and a handle or knot on the other, and is usually anywhere from 20-50 feet in length. I recommend 40 foot long lines because they provide the dog the option of moving around quite a bit while not becoming unwieldy to manage. These tools give your dog more opportunity to exercise in fields and parks without having to take walks in places which might be difficult for the dog to go.

McDevitt, Leslie: A positive dog trainer in the Philadelphia area. She frequently works with sports dogs and reactivity. She created the game, "Look at that!" for helping dogs to tolerate the presence of a dog. In our classes, we often call it, "Where's the dog?" More information on this game is available in her book, *Control Unleashed: From Stress to Confidence, From Distraction to Focus*, 2007, Clean Run Productions.

Natural Reward: Many trainers call these, "life rewards"; these are things that the dog really wants to do. Sniffing is a good example. If the dog pulls to get to a sniffing spot, stop and wait for him to look at you, then click and tell him to go sniff. Other examples are getting into the car, access to a stream or pond, or access to a favorite person or dog. Using these rewards to your benefit increases your dogs' desire to check in with you when he wants something.

Negative Punishment: The removal of things that the dog finds rewarding in response to a behavior that we want to decrease. This is best paired with positive reinforcement for behaviors we want to increase. An example of this is when the dog jumps on the person for attention: the person should walk away and ignore the dog, but come back shortly thereafter and ask the dog to sit, so he can reward the dog for doing something we want to increase (sitting).

Negative Reinforcement: The removal of something the dog perceives as aversive in response to a behavior you want to increase. The simplest example is the use of the choke chain. When the dog is forging while heeling, the person applies pressure with the choke chain; the dog doesn't care for this, and returns to heel position to make the choking stop. The dog is heeling to avoid the correction. Note that the dog is not heeling because working with the person is fun...this is not a technique we want to use! In this example, the application of the choking with the choke chain involves the use of positive punishment, as well. Confusing, isn't it?

Operant Conditioning: A style of learning in which the subject actively *operates* on his environment in order to get rewards. This concept was made famous by B.F. Skinner. The dog tries to figure out what it takes to "get the good stuff." We call this a *thinking dog* as opposed to a *reacting dog*. Clicker training uses operant conditioning.

Parallel Walking: An activity we often use in our classes when working on dog-dog reactivity. It involves two or more dogs walking in the same direction, at more or less the same speed. We begin by having the dogs at a distance from each other that is big enough so that they do not react to each other. The humans can click and treat a number of things; loose leash walking, looking at the handler, turning away from the other dog, or anything else that the human likes which the dog is doing. By keeping the dog subthreshold and by using operant conditioning, the dog practices remaining in a thinking mode rather than a reacting mode. The distance between the dogs is gradually decreased.

Positive Punishment: The application of something that the dog perceives as aversive in response to a behavior we want to diminish. This can be anything from striking to simply giving the dog a look of disapproval. It is important to understand that it's the dog's perception of what is aversive, not the human's perception.

Positive Reinforcement: The application of something that the dog perceives as good in response to a behavior we want to increase. We generally divide this into two categories, primary reinforcers and secondary reinforcers (see definitions).

Post-Reinforcement Dip: The lack of attention immediately following the delivery of a reward. Once the dog has been clicked and treated, his attention may wander; it is the period of time after he received a reward and before being asked to do something else. This is a particularly dangerous time for a reactive dog, as it is prime time for finding something to react to! Often, I will recommend rapid-fire clicks and treats for a single behavior to highly reward it, and then fade the frequency over time.

Pow-Wow: The term I use to describe the meetings we sometimes have at the beginning of reactive class. Here, we are able to discuss our dogs' progress and setbacks during the past week, discuss important terms and concepts, and choreograph our activities for the class. More recently, we have done most of this work online via our chat group.

Premack Principle: In operant conditioning, the principle that, given a higher-probability behavior and a lower-probability behavior, a person could ask her dog to do a lower-probability behavior and use the higher-probability behavior as a reward. This increases the chance that the dog will do the lower-probability behavior

Primary Reinforcer: things that are necessary for survival; namely, food, water, air, shelter, and sex. While all of these things have been used in the training of exotic and zoo animals, food is the easiest (and most ethical) reinforcer to use with dogs. Using food also allows for rapid repetitions when teaching new skills.

Reactivity: Fear and/or anxiety-driven behavior wherein the dog reacts with much greater intensity to certain stimuli than one would think necessary. A dog can be reactive to people, dogs or objects. Most often, the behavior looks like aggression, but its purpose is to drive away the fear-causing stimulus.

Secondary Reinforcer: Things that are not necessary for survival but through association with primary reinforcers, become rewarding in themselves. In humans, money is a great example of a secondary reinforcer. While almost anything can become a secondary reinforcer (also known as a conditioned reinforcer) if paired repeatedly with a primary reinforcer (also known as an unconditioned reinforcer), the ones most often used with dogs are praise, play and touch. It is very important to note that many dogs do not like to be touched in ways that humans touch them, so make sure you explore what your dog really likes before using it as a secondary reinforcer!

Send-Offs: An activity in which the dog learns to approach people in a mannerly fashion. The handler starts with the dog sitting on one side of him (usually the left), facing the same direction as the handler. The handler then *sends the dog off* to a person who is standing six to ten feet away from them, facing them. As he is *sending off* the dog, the handler says, "Go see," or something to that effect, while sending the dog with his pointer finger pointing at the visiting person. The visiting person *meets* his pointer finger to the handler's finger, so the dog has the most obvious direction possible. The visitor then draws his arm toward himself, and as the dog comes toward him, he asks the dog to sit. The visitor then clicks and treats the dog. When the person is finished visiting the dog (he can ask the dog to do other skills while visiting, or work on petting by touching the dog in an increasing intensity over time while clicking and treating), he sends the dog back to the handler. This activity is incredibly valuable, but must be taken very slowly for many dogs. There are many opportunities to overstimulate a reactive dog with this activity.

Separation Anxiety: A behavior problem in which the dog goes into a panic when the owner leaves or acts as if he's going to leave. Symptoms of separation anxiety include but are not limited to pacing, panting, drooling, foaming, crying, whining, urination, defecating, vomiting, digging at entries and exits, often breaking nails in the process, trying to eat through exits, often bloodying the mouth in the process. There is a spectrum of intensity that covers separation anxiety. Very severe cases may involve a dog jumping through a plate-glass window. The best possible treatment is behavioral and can often include the use of DAP® (Dog Appeasing Pheromone, brand name "Comfort Zone®"), homeopathic remedies, herbal remedies, or anxiolytic drugs (via prescription from your vet).

Storm Defender™ Cape (www.stormdefender.com): A cape with a metal mesh lining which is placed on a dog during electrical storms. It can help to discharge the dog's fur and shields him from the static charge buildup, reducing his sensitivity to the charge.

Stuff-A-Dog: A classical conditioning activity wherein the person places a treat in her dog's mouth while saying her dog's name. Each time she says the dog's name, the intonation should be varied to accommodate the different ways in which she might say her dog's name (happy, angry, loud, quiet, sad, silly, frustrated, panicked), and she should do a stuff-a-dog every three to five seconds. The occasional nickname can be added to the mix. Because there is no conscious learning take place on the part of the dog, the person will need to do about 5000 repetitions of stuff-a-dog. The goals for this activity are to increase name recognition, focus, and recall.

Subsidence: The phenomenon wherein a dog perceives a fearful stimulus paired with a highly pleasant stimulus, and the result is that the dog is more able to tolerate the fearful stimulus. The theory is that the pleasant association diminishes the fearful association, i.e., causes the fear to *subside*. This term was coined by Tara Walters, a student in my reactive class, and came about after many unsuccessful attempts on my part to find a pre-existing term to label the concept.

Subthreshold: A dog is considered *subthreshold* when his arousal level is still low enough that he can think and process. The threshold is the point at which the dog will switch from using operant behavior to reactive behavior. The goal for working with a reactive dog is to always keep him subthreshold, while occasionally bumping up his threshold. That is to say, I want to push the dog just to the point where it's tough for him to think and respond, but is still able to do so. Go too far and he'll blow, or go *superthreshold.* By doing this the dog's ability to remain in thinking mode increases with the distraction level over time.

Sudden Environmental Contrast: The behavioral tendency of a dog to react intensely to stimuli which appear suddenly or out of context. In some ways, this may seem to parallel a startle response. However, the intensity of the dog's reaction is more intense than necessary from a survival perspective. An example: Acacia is walking on a hiking trail. Around a bend in the trail comes a person with a dog. Acacia growls, barks, and rushes up to the strangers. But at a dog show, where there are hundreds of dogs and people, Acacia's behavior is calm and she ignores others. This is probably a stress response, and I theorize that it has a genetic component.

Targeting: An operant conditioning skill where the dog has learned to touch something in order to get a reward. The target object is usually a finger or hand, but it can be any other object or anything a finger or hand points to. The dog can target with any body part, but it is usually his nose.

Ten-Second Rule: The dog has ten seconds from the time he is asked to do something to actually do it. As soon as the person asks the dog to do something, he begins to count to himself. If the dog responds within ten seconds, the dog gets clicked and treated. If the person counts to ten, the dog goes back into the car/crate without any interaction at all – no commentary, no emotion. The function of this response is to provide negative punishment for a lack of focus on the person. Over time, the dog has fewer seconds in which to respond: once he is able to respond consistently within ten seconds, the time goes down to eight seconds, then six, then five. I believe it's fair to allow the dog four to five seconds to look around his environment before checking in with his person.

Verbal Marker: The use of a word to mark the behavior a person is looking for in his dog. The word ought to be one or two syllables, should not be something he often says in other circumstances, and should be spoken exactly the same way each time. I suggest using words such as, "Yay!", "Perfect!", "Super!", or "Bravo!" rather than, "Yes," "Good," or "Okay." The marker can be changed, and over time, the dog learns that the energy put into saying the marker is the lowest common denominator. The verbal marker is followed by a treat, just as would be done with a clicker.

Wait: The concept which means "no forward motion" to the dog. This is different from *stay* in that body posture movements are fine, so long as the dog doesn't make any forward progress. Of course, this is a matter of personal preference, and some folks use the *stay* cue instead or interchangeably. I usually begin by teaching this concept in relation to entrances and exits, most notably the car. It is absolutely critical as the owner of a reactive dog for the owner to know exactly what's going on outside before the dog knows. This is management and provides great opportunities for training, as well.

To teach this, begin with your dog in the car. You will notice that when a dog has the intent of moving forward (as in to jump out of the car), his head will move forward and down. Counteract this motion by placing a treat in his mouth while applying gentle pressure backward as he takes the treat, releasing the treat when his head returns to a neutral position. While you are doing this, say, "Wait." This is the classical conditioning approach and is usually the way I start to teach this skill. Once the dog begins to make this association, you can start to add a hand signal to the cue (I use the pointer finger in an upward position), and then you can begin to add duration and the distance you travel from your dog for distraction.

Whale Eye: A description of a dog's eye expression when he is under great stress. In my last book, I used the phrase, "dinner plate eyeballs" for the same behavior. The dog's bottom lid is drawn down to expose the white of the eye. This is usually a sign that the dog is extremely uncomfortable and might feel the need to take some precaution. In many cases, the next behavior the dog emits is to snap at the source of stress. Whale eye is indicative of the immediate need to remove the dog from the stressful situation.

Acknowledgements

Not only does any worthy project take time, it also requires the assistance of many people. Sometimes those people don't realize that they are helping or how much they are helping, but when that project is complete, acknowledgement is due. Occasionally, the assistance is offered, and other times it is requested. It is equally valuable in each case.

To my students (and their families), both human and canine, in the reactive class: Kim, Don, DJ and Mollie; Kristen, Linda and Bailey; Marie, Mark and Yankee; Laura and Spencer; Colleen, Tracy and Maggie; Patti, Tara, Glen and Max; Christi, Pat and Shadow; Deb and Elvis; Lisa and Indy. You reinforce my belief that it is worth having faith in your dog, in your relationship with your dog, and in the ability of behavioral science to gain real, lasting, and tangible results. Your dedication to your dogs and to this class validates my work. I give more to this class than to any other class I teach, and it's always worth it.

To my husband, Pete Smoyer, who is unfailing in his dedication to my cause. You are always there to get me the things I forgot, fix the things I broke, walk the dogs when I run out of time, act as kennel help at shows, get me the directions when I'm hopelessly lost, feed me three square because I'm too frantic to do it myself, publish my books, produce my videos…all without complaint. Oh, and scratch my back! You deserve a medal, not just for all of those things, but also for being a loving husband and my best friend.

To Susan Sanders, my associate trainer for my other classes, who has been tremendously supportive through this very difficult year. As if undertaking this book project wasn't challenging enough, Pete and I had to deal with the purchase of our new property, the deaths of both of our fathers and both of our older dogs, all within six months. Sue, I couldn't have muddled through without your faith, love and support. One true friend opens the other's eyes (and sometimes keeps her friend's eyes open) to the talents she has. This, you have done for me, and I hope I have done this for you.

To Tess Stinson, for helping me to proof a work in progress, and to staunchly insist that I hung the moon, despite my excessive use of commas and parentheses!

To Mom, Evelyn H. Brown and to sister, Katy Fischer and her husband, Eric Fischer, for remaining interested in my writing and training adventures despite this past difficult year.

To truly positive dog trainers everywhere, for being positive and for staunchly refusing to use positive punishment and/or negative reinforcement simply because it might be quicker or easier. We all know that the dogs appreciate this, even if they can't tell us. We also all know that we are taking the more ethical route, and we know that criticism is one of the early steps toward change. Let's stay the course and one day our techniques will be status quo.

Finally, to Acacia (Canadian Ch. ARCH Bellsha Borae Prairie Fire, HIC, CGC, TDI, R1 MCL, R2 MCL, RL3, RN, RL1X, RL2X). You taught me to have patience, to remain neutral in emotion, and to make sense of all that behavioral stuff I learned in graduate school! As if that weren't enough, you teach other dogs every day. You are my partner in this cause, and while I know you love your work, I still must thank you for being willing to do so. I hope we have many more years of work together, and even more years of love.

Resources and Reading

Behavioral Books:

Aloff, Brenda. *Canine Body Language, A Photographic Guide*. Wenatchee WA: Dogwise Publishing, 2005.

Brown, Ali. *Scaredy Dog! Understanding and Rehabilitating Your Reactive Dog*. Allentown, PA: Tanacacia Press, 2004.

Donaldson, Jean. *Dogs Are From Neptune*. Montreal: Lasar Multimedia Productions, 1998.

McConnell, Patricia. *The Cautious Canine*. Black Earth, WI: Dog's Best Friend, Ltd., 2002.

———. *I'll Be Home Soon! How to Prevent and Treat Separation Anxiety*. Black Earth, WI: Dog's Best Friend, Ltd., 2000.

McDevitt, Leslie. *Control Unleashed: From Stress to Confidence, From Distraction to Focus*. South Hadley, MA: Clean Run Productions, 2007.

Rugaas, Turid. *On Talking Terms with Dogs: Calming Signals*. Wenatchee, WA: Dogwise Publishing, 2006.

Sapolsky, Robert M. *Why Zebras Don't Get Ulcers, An Updated Guide to Stress, Stress-Related Diseases, and Coping*. New York: Henry Holt and Company, LLC, 1998.

General Books:

Clothier, Suzanne. *Bones Would Rain from the Sky.* New York: Warner Books, 2002.

Coppinger, Raymond and Lorna. *Dogs: A Startling New Understanding of Canine Origin, Behavior and Evolution.* New York: Scribner, 2001.

Donaldson, Jean. *The Culture Clash.* Berkeley: James & Kenneth Publishers, 1996.

Fogle, Bruce. The Dog's Mind. New York: Howel Book House, 1990

McConnell, Patricia. *The Other End of the Leash.* New York: Ballantine Books, 2002.

Miller, Pat. *The Power of Positive Dog Training.* New York: Wiley Publishing, 2001

———. *Positive Perspectives: Love Your Dog, Train Your Dog.* Wenatchee WA: Dogwise Publishing, 2004.

O'Driscoll, Catherine. *Shock to the System.* Wenatchee, WA: Dogwise Publishing, 2005.

Prior, Karen. *Don't Shoot the Dog.* New York: Bantam Books, 1999.

Tools and Websites:

Bach's Flower Essences: www.bachcentre.com/centre/bfrani.htm

TTouch: www.tteam-ttouch.com/

Storm Defender Cape: www.stormdefender.com/

DAP: www.petcomfortzone.com/czdogs.htm

Anxiety Wrap: www.anxietywrap.com/

Calming Cap: www.premier.com

Books: www.dogwise.com

Trainers: www.apdt.com

Clickers: www.clickertraining.com or www.sitstay.com

Thyroid Testing: Dr. Jean Dodds and Hemopet, www.itsfortheanimals.com/HEMOPET.HTM, or see www.hemopet.com

Kong: www.kongcompany.com

Index